text by Chiara Piroddi

WHITE STAR PUBLISHERS

WS White Star Publishers® is a registered trademark property
of White Star s.r.l.

© 2019 White Star s.r.l.
Piazzale Luigi Cadorna, 6 - 20123 Milan, Italy
www.whitestar.it

Translation: Irina Oryshkevich – Editing: Inga Sempel

ISBN 978-88-544-1382-5
 2 3 4 5 6   24 23 22 21 20

Printed in Poland

MONTESSORI
LAB AT HOME

A practical guide to the Montessori Teaching Method

Contents

Introduction

Educating a child is a challenge as important as it is complex. Nowadays a child has at their disposal all sorts of stimuli to practice and develop their cognitive skills. But which are the best methods and the most appropriate materials for promoting such development? Which educational method is the most effective for a child?

Maria Montessori came up with her own pedagogical method by reflecting on the true purpose of a child's education, which is regarded as of inestimable value for society; it represents an opportunity for building a better and more peaceful world.

"The child is endowed with unknown powers that can open them to a bright future. If rebuilding is truly the aim, then the objective of education must be to develop the human potential." The child has a boundless cognitive and emotional potential that can best express itself if nurtured within a relationship made of trust, respect and unconditional love.

According to Montessori, an informed adult who's aware of their limitations and resources, knows how to approach their child in the role of a patient observer, an expert model and a loving guide, thus creating the best conditions for the child to develop confidence, sense of self-efficacy and autonomy.

Inspired by the principles of the Montessori method, this book is intended as a practical guide where parents of children of age 1-5 will be able to find stimulating prompts as well as practical suggestions for indoor and outdoor activities, all aimed at best promoting the development of the child's potential and encouraging their autonomy and self-confidence. After a brief summary on the origins and aspects of the Montessori method, parents will find suggestions on how to recognize their children's learning windows, which attitude to adopt in group play, which types of fun activities to create and propose, how to adapt the Montessori principles to commercially available games and how to create a home environment suited to the needs of their child.

The Montessori approach will reveal to be easy and accessible to everyone, thanks to concrete examples, explanatory illustrations, as well as tips and strategies for applying it in a simple way in any home and into one's own daily routine.

Historical Background

Maria Montessori and the birth of a new pedagogy

Maria Tecla Artemisia Montessori was born in Chiaravalle, near Ancona, on August 31st 1870. A woman of many interests, determined, with an extraordinary intelligence and a love for scientific research, she was the first Italian woman to graduate from Medical School. She conducted studies in Pedagogy, Neuropsychiatry and Anthropology and was constantly advancing her ideals as a fervent feminist. She always led her life at the forefront of social and cultural issues, devoting herself to the poorest sectors of society and to women's rights. A champion of women's emancipation and peace manifestos, she never took political sides; instead she addressed political leaders with ideas and innovative solutions that would improve society.

Her passion for knowledge, her initiative, her sensitivity to social and political issues and her love for children led her to travel a great deal across Europe and the United States and to spend her entire life between studies and research, thus bequeathing an immense cultural legacy of knowledge about the child and education methods to the whole of mankind.

Maria Montessori grew up in a Catholic middle-class family, embracing the liberal ideas of the Risorgimento and the battle against totalitarianism. Her father, Alessandro Montessori, originally from Ferrara, was an official at the Ministry of Finance. Her mother, Renilde Stoppani, from Marche, came from a family of small landowners. However, one of the most important figures in her life was her uncle Antonio Stoppani, an abbot and scientist committed to demonstrate the coexistence of faith and science. The young Maria Montessori identified Abbot Stoppani as the point of reference who inspired her to nurture her studies and her passion for knowledge.

She spent her childhood between Florence and Rome, where she settled with her family in 1875. She immediately showed great propensity for study and intellectual disciplines and initially directed her attention towards engineering.

For this reason, from 1883 to 1886 she devoted herself to technical studies, a choice that soon proved unsuitable to her inclinations. After graduation came the first confrontations with her father, who wanted his daughter to follow a career as a teacher. Unfortunately her father's plans were ill-matched with the interests of the young and enterprising Maria, who instead burned with the desire to dedicate herself to biological science.

At the time, however, enrolment in the Faculty of Medicine was reserved exclusively to the students of the Classical Lyceum. Therefore, she had to enrol in the Faculty of Sciences in 1890 and move on to the Faculty of Medicine two years later. But her talent did not take long to reveal itself.

SHOWN HERE IS MARIA MONTESSORI AMONGST YOUNG PUPILS OF A SCHOOL IN LONDON IN 1951, WHEN THE SUCCESS OF HER METHOD HAD ALREADY SPREAD FAR AND WIDE ON AN INTERNATIONAL SCALE.

She graduated brilliantly, becoming the third Italian woman to achieve such an academic accomplishment, which had always been the prerogative of male students.

In 1895, after earning her degree in Medicine, she met her colleague Giuseppe Montesano (with whom she would later have a son, Mario), and from this encounter arose her decision to specialize in Neuropsychiatry at the Psychiatric Clinic at the University of Rome. That's how her course of studies as a research scientist began, focusing initially on bacteria and diseases in Rome's poorest neighborhoods, and afterwards on mental illness.

Around 1900, she began conducting research at the Roman Psychiatric Asylum of S. Maria della Pietà, that hosted children with disabilities and behavioral disorders left in a state of serious emotional deprivation, along with adults suffering from psychiatric illnesses. Montessori devoted herself to these children with love and deep humane attention, realizing quite soon that the educational method used at the asylum was ill-suited to the needs and psychophysical abilities of those young children.

She therefore began developing a deep interest in children with mental disabilities, turning to the works of Jean-Marc-Gaspard Itard and Edouard Séguin, who were amongst her greatest sources of inspiration.

In the meantime, political struggles for civil rights and social conquests were spreading across the world. Maria Montessori began to take an interest in the emancipation of women and, in 1896, took part in the first Congress of the International Council of Women on women's rights in Berlin.

Throughout her life, she continued her battle for women's rights, always placing herself at the forefront of feminist protests and conferences. On March 31st 1898, she secretly gave birth to her son Mario, born to her relationship with Montesano. Their relationship remained clandestine for a long time as it would not have been well received in the scientific community. As a result, the son too had to be delivered in secret and was immediately handed over to foster care. She regained custody only in 1913.

In September 1898, Montessori participated in the Pedagogical Congress of Turin, where she delivered an important lecture on the relationship between Medicine and Pedagogy and first spoke about a special education targeted at children with mental problems, thus trying to raise public interest in the topic.

She got what she desired; in 1906, a nursery school for working class children living in Rome's new council apartment blocks was commissioned. The first Children's Houses thus came into existence, putting into effect Montessori's experience in education. The first House opened on 6th January 1907, the second on April 7th of the same year, and in 1908 another was opened in Milan by her faithful pupil, Anna Maria Maccheroni. This new school structure was organized and furnished in such a way as to make the child feel as though it was their own, hence the term "Children's" house.

After the terrible earthquake that struck Messina and Reggio Calabria, a fourth Children's House was opened in 1908 to house orphan children in Rome, near the convent of the Franciscan Missionary Sisters of Mary, where they introduced practical everyday activities, which would later become central to the Montessori method.

Out of all these experiences was born Montessori's first and most important work in 1909, "The method of scientific pedagogy applied to childhood education in the Children's Houses". Destined to a great and long-lasting worldwide success, the book discussed in-

novative concepts and revolutionary methods, such as the education of the senses through organic materials, the recognition of the child's freedom and the respect for them and the opposition to the teacher's practice of transfering knowledge to the pupils by using rewards and punishments. Instead of the traditional methods that included reading and repeating by heart, the Montessori method promoted children's learning through the use of physical tools, thus leading to far better results.

The Montessori method was introduced in a primary school for the first time in 1910 and was extended to very young children in 1920. Maria Montessori thus created two distinct places: the Nursery, for infants 2-15 months of age, and the Children's Community, for children aged 15 months to 2 and a half years.

The reputation of the Montessori approach soon traveled overseas; several American educators began coming to Italy to visit the Children's Houses to then recreate them in the United States.

IN THE 1920S, GARDENING AND CARING FOR SMALL ANIMALS WERE INNOVATIVE METHODS TO TEACH THE LOVE FOR NATURE TO YOUNG CHILDREN AT A MONTESSORI SCHOOL.

Montessori's written work was distributed in 58 countries and was translated into 36 languages. Montessori-oriented associations of educators were soon established; amongst the first ones were the Montessori Society of Scotland, the British Montessori Society and the American Montessori Society. In Italy, a National Montessori Committee was founded in 1916 too.

In 1915 Montessori settled down in Spain, as her pupil Maccheroni had opened a Children's House in Barcelona. During her experience in Catalonia, Montessori expanded her method by applying it to Catholic education, so much so that a child-size chapel was constructed specifically for infants at the Escola Modelo Montessori in Barcelona. She then produced more works about the role of spirituality within the method.

In 1922 Montessori was appointed supervisor of Italy's Montessori schools, and the Montessori method was introduced to 20 primary schools in Naples.

At first Italy's rising fascist regime was sympathetic and supportive of Montessori's activity, appreciating the publicity it enjoyed abroad. Indeed, Gentile's reform anticipated the possibility of adopting the Montessori method to schools. Mussolini himself contacted the pedagogist and assured her of his support. The National Montessori Institute was established with bases in Rome and Naples, with the mission of authorizing the publication of books and the establishment of new schools, manufacturing the "Montessori materials" destined to the schools and organizing courses for educators.

The International Montessori Association (AMI), with its headquarters in Rome, was founded in 1929, with the support of notable figures, such as Sigmund Freud and Jean Piaget.

But Montessori's dream could not go hand in hand with a totalitarian era; the unrestrainable need for freedom and the universalistic inclination towards peace, which lay at the heart of the Montessori pedagogy were considered pure folly by the Nazi regime. The political and cultural crisis exploded, and the Montessori schools were shut down both in Italy and in Germany. In 1935 the AMI headquarters had to move to Amsterdam. Maria Montessori sought refuge with her son in Spain, where she secretly continued to publish her works. In 1934, while in Barcelona, she published several volumes documenting the results of her experience at Rome's School of Method, Psycho-Arithmetic and Psycho-Geometry. The Italian translation of *Il bambino in famiglia* [*The Child in the Family*] came out in 1936, as did the French version of

In this Montessori school in Berlin, the study of letters and the composition of words are being tackled with the help of tactile materials, similar in terms of their use to those described on page 60.

The Secret of Childhood, which appeared in Italian only in 1938 in Switzerland.

In 1936 the onset of the Spanish Civil War forced the Montessori family to move again, first to England then to the Netherlands; in 1939, they traveled to India. Here she once again saw Gandhi, whom she had already met in London and with whom she shared ideas on the need to change society and guide it towards peace. In India, Montessori led a course for Indian teachers and had the opportunity to immerse herself in Indian culture and live close to nature. This inspired her to formulate a new concept: the cosmic education, with the purpose of kindling and developing knowledge and love for nature, animals, peace, and life itself. Gardening and, wherever possible, the care of small animals were therefore introduced into Montessori schools.

The outbreak of World War II forced Montessori to remain in India, where she continued her studies on the newborn's development and on the child's mind, publishing *How to Bring Out Human Potential* in 1947, and *The Absorbent Mind* in 1949.

In 1947, once the war had ended, Maria Montessori returned to Italy to reorganize the Montessori Association and reopen the Montessori schools, but kept her main residence in Amsterdam and continued to travel around the world. Her fame was at its peak and she was even nominated for the Nobel Peace Prize (her writings on educating to peace are compiled in the volume, *Education and Peace*, Milan 1949).

She died on May 6th 1952 in Noordwijk aan Zee (Holland), buried in the local Catholic Cemetery.

The Montessori system has been recognized as a valuable and highly effective educational and didactic method worldwide, regardless of culture or religion: around 65,000 Montessori schools and institutes are estimated to exist in the world.

The United States has 4,500 institutes, while in Asia schools exist all over the continent, from Turkey to Saudi Arabia, from India to China, from Thailand to Vietnam, from Korea to Japan. In Africa there are a number of Montessori schools in Morocco, Senegal, Nigeria, Tanzania, Namibia and South Africa. About 2,800 schools are also in Europe, situated in practically every nation, including Russia and several Republics of the former Soviet Union. They are definitely mostly widespread in the Anglo-Saxon and Scandinavian nations, which have always placed much weight on the role of children's education within society.

In Italy, on the other hand, where Montessori schools are still scarce, there are barely 200.

The Montessori View

A new pedagogy

"Education must be intended as an aid to the development of innate psychic powers within the human individual."

Maria Montessori was undoubtedly a pioneer of an important cultural revolution within the field of pedagogy. Her goal was to attain change in mankind, starting from the beginning, i.e. from the way a child is educated. Thanks to her empirical attitude, she tried to promote a scientific pedagogy, based on direct observation and objective feedback. Starting with anthropological studies and experimental psychology, she spent most of her life observing children and the spontaneous changes in them, believing that *"a fundamental cornerstone of scientific pedagogy should be a school that allows the child's spontaneous expressions and personal vivaciousness."*

Montessori brought attention to the need for social change, for a renewal in human relations, especially deteriorated by totalitarian systems. At the basis of her thought process lay the idea of an oppressive society that left no room for freedom of expression and had no faith in natural human development, but instead expected to cage and guide people in the deluded belief that it could control them. She firmly believed that the pedagogical methods that were in vogue at the time led to "the eclipse and death of natural life and to the suffocation of the child's spontaneous creativity."

Her way of thinking is therefore more than just a method; it's a genuine pedagogical approach, aimed at promoting change in the human being, in the belief that children raised with love and respect for their personality and their freedom can become responsible and trustworthy adults, capable of rediscovering moral values.

THE LIFE TRAVELER

"The magnificence of the human personality begins with a person's birth. Such a statement leads to a conclusion that may seem strange: education should start at birth."

Let's begin with a consideration: how many of us have ever thought that a newborn can already be considered an individual endowed with a psychic life, with ideas, innate abilities, curiosity for the environment and a vital force? For some, perhaps, this is a concept that runs a bit against the tide; even today there is a tendency to believe that an infant is nothing more than a soft cuddly body that needs washing, feeding and sleep, in accordance with our routine and our needs — almost a puppy to train.

Yet, a century ago, Maria Montessori had a radically different vision, where the child was the center of society and the beneficiary of a profound cultural reflection. Against the view of a newborn as inert, she believed the baby to have significant psychic abilities even from the first hours of life. *"Every being that comes into the world not only is a physical body; it also possesses latent functions that are not those of their physiological organs, but those that depend on instinct."*

She was convinced that the child has an imprisoned soul, which constantly tries to emerge, to make itself visible and grow, irradiating life to the different parts of the body and thus generating movement, which is essential to learning.

The Montessorian philosophy opened up to the great importance of pedagogical studies of the early years in a child's life. Pedagogy had previously regarded the child as *"socially non-existent in itself,"* weak and therefore assisted by the adult. On the contrary, Maria Montessori observed that the foundations of the adult that the child will become in the future, are laid in the first three years of life. The child's great virtues and innate abilities can find fertile ground for expression within a welcoming and spontaneous environment. The child is endowed with an absorbent mind, i.e. with the mental ability to absorb the lessons deriving from their own direct experiences with in-credible speed and readiness, and thus generate patterns of actions and behaviors.

A Montessori education therefore begins with the first encounter between the baby and their parents, with their first discovery of the world, at a moment when behavior is at its most instinctive and spontaneous, solely dictated by the laws of nature. If the adult stops and observes the newborn, they can discover a world of opportunities not to be wasted, but which should be their responsibility to seize and develop.

The child is by nature a passionate explorer of their surroundings and instinctively directs themselves to it. *"A child is like a life traveler,"* claims Montessori, *"who looks around at the new things presented to them and tries to understand the unknown language of the people around them, making grand and spontaneous efforts to understand and imitate them."*

EDUCATE TO FREEDOM WITH DISCIPLINE

"An individual who has been artificially rendered silent isn't necessarily disciplined. Such an individual is annihilated, not disciplined."

Agreeing with the Montessori view may seem complex at first, because it appears conflicting with what our culture has conveyed to us over the years, by interpreting education as some kind of power game between an adult in charge of knowledge – the educator – and a shapeless, malleable human being – the to-be-educated individual.

According to the Montessori approach, however, education is not the one dogmatically passed on by the teacher, but rather a *natural process* that unfolds by virtue of spontaneous experiences within one's own environment.

Montessori firmly believes that the child needs **freedom**, which is necessary for developing the creativity that the child naturally possesses, but which is repressed by the rules of society and the continuous interventions of adults. From this freedom arises *re-sponsibility*, which brings discipline. Freedom and discipline would appear to be two antithetical concepts incapable of coexisting, but Montessori made them closely related: *"we define as disciplined an individual who is their own master, capable of self-determination when the decision about following a rule of life arises."*

Does that mean that a child enjoys the possibility of unlimited actions? Not at all. The child's freedom is limited by collective interest; for this reason, the educational plan encompasses an exercise in self-control towards all those forms of behavior that somehow harm others or are socially improper.

And what about the adult? What is their role within a freedom-based educational system? The adult must intervene to help the child secure that freedom. This means that their intervention is reduced to a minimum; being considerate and respectful of the child's phases, never intrusive or inhibiting, never anticipating the child nor taking their place. The adult's intervention is measured, since an excessive assistance has

THE FOUR STAGES OF DEVELOPMENT

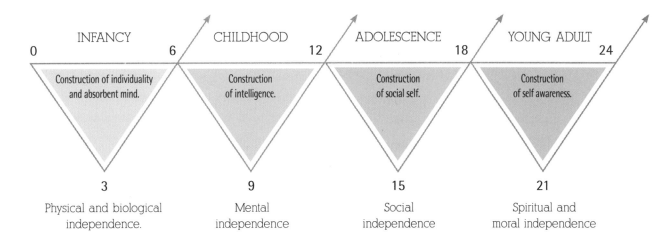

INFANCY	CHILDHOOD	ADOLESCENCE	YOUNG ADULT
0 ... 6	6 ... 12	12 ... 18	18 ... 24
Construction of individuality and absorbent mind.	Construction of intelligence.	Construction of social self.	Construction of self awareness.
3	9	15	21
Physical and biological independence.	Mental independence	Social independence	Spiritual and moral independence

the negative effect of denying the possibility of expression. They adopt a role of guide and supporter and demonstrate a good deal of patience and power of observation.

Described this way, it appears as an extraordinary method; but what happens in actual practice? Don't worry, we will talk about that.

THE FOUR STAGES OF DEVELOPMENT

"Development is a succession of births."

The Montessori education project is built on a holistic vision of the human being that takes into consideration the physical, emotional and intellectual characteristics of the person at various stages of their life, from birth to adulthood - at around age 24.

Maria Montessori identified four major periods or stages in a person's development, each one with its own peculiarities. Knowing these developmental stages allows us to better understand the needs that arise from time to time in the infant-child-adolescent-young adult and to most effectively intervene to promote the development of their potential.

The diagram above shows the various stages and indicates the approximate age ranges covered by them.

The use of the triangle to illustrate each phase symbolizes that each period goes through a phase of growth and maximum expression of need, which is followed by a gradual deceleration, to eventually give way to the next stage and therefore to different needs. Let's look at the 4 stages in greater detail.

STAGE 1 – AGE 0 TO 6: THE ABSORBENT MIND

This is the phase that corresponds to infancy and the progressive creation of the person as an individual.

Throughout this stage, the child's mind is like a sponge that absorbs everything from the environment. The child has a high sensitivity to context, so high that everything in their surroundings awakens their interest and enthusiasm to such an extent that the regions of their brain are activated and their body undergoes a transformation. *"The child undergoes a transformation,"* writes Montessori, *"Impressions not only penetrate but also shape their mind."* The most significant example is that of language. The child just needs to be exposed to the sound of languages for their mind to gradually learn their phonological, grammatical, and syntactic structure, and reproduce language in an increasingly accurate way.

During this phase, the child is characterized by particular innate sensibilities, i.e. the sensitive periods, which we will explain more in depth later on.

The needs that are relevant to 0-6 year old children pertain to the construction of autonomy: the child wishes to act on their own and seeks **physical independence**.

The adult's task will therefore be to help the child reach such an objective, by making them capable of performing various actions autonomously; the child will free themselves from external assistance, identifying as a separate and independent individual. All those activities relating to **practical life** - through which children learn to take care of themselves and of their surroundings - should therefore be encouraged.

2ND STAGE - AGE 6 TO 12: THE CONSTRUCTION OF INTELLIGENCE

This is the phase of childhood, when the child is considered to be sufficiently prepared to face a more structured learning context, such as that one of school. The child understands, listens to the teacher, questions him or her and moves through the world guided by their first logical deductions and reflections. The child now has an intense thirst for knowledge and therefore loves to explore the world of science and nature, and seeks logical explanation for the phenomena around them. It is at this stage that the important transition from concrete to **abstract thought** takes place. For this reason, the child also begins to have an attraction for what is not physically perceptible, therefore activating their imagination, inventing stories, and using their creativity to fantasize. At this stage, the child wants to think autonomously and seeks **intellectual independence**.

3RD STAGE - AGE 12 TO 18: THE CONSTRUCTION OF THE SOCIAL SELF

This is the daunting phase of adolescence, when children seem to radically change their identity, becoming disagreeable, eccentric, unstable and passionate, agonizingly searching for what they want to be.

At this stage, the adolescent's primary need is to search for his or her autonomy from a conceptual point of view - i.e. come up with a personal way of thinking - but also find **emotional independence**, that is feeling less dependent on their parents' assistance.

The adolescent needs to test themselves outside the nucleus of the family, needs to build friendships, cultivate a feeling of belonging to groups beyond the family and often in opposition to it, as if to test the flavor of a new, different reality. Their cultural interest deepens; they are thirsty for knowledge and desire to explore it more in depth. As they assign more importance to social and moral values, the adolescent's moral conscience begins to ripen. In this phase, the adult's role is difficult and delicate; it is based on the constant mediation of the adolescent's antithetical demands for autonomy and protection.

4TH STAGE - AGE 18 TO 24: CONSTRUCTION OF SELF-AWARENESS

This final phase leads to an adjustment and to the attainment of balance. After the restless quest for their own identity, the adolescent has developed their own conscience, their own way of thinking about the world and about themselves and has set goals and ideals. This period sees the formation of a personal scale of values, the identification of what is right and what is wrong. The adolescent is now ready to establish their place in the world, outside the original family.

THE SENSITIVE PERIODS

"If the child has not been able to act according to the guidelines of their sensitive period, the opportunity for a natural achievement has been lost. Lost forever."

During their development, the child goes through certain stages associated with a greater and specific sensitivity for certain types of stimuli: Montessori calls these the *sensory periods*. These represent some sort of natural, instinctive and irresistible signal for the child, a guide that makes them more receptive to certain impulses and elements within the environment. During these stages, the adult ought to make sure to provide the child with the type of stimulus to which they are more receptive, in order to encourage their growth and the development of their skills. The window for acquiring skills is limited; once it closes, the ability to acquire that given mental skill becomes more difficult. Languages are a typical example; the

child is most receptive to language up to the age of 6-7, after which this window of sensitivity changes and the ease of acquisition decreases. If we want our child to learn more languages, it is better to expose them to multilingualism when they still are at a pre-scholastic age, and their learning process is simple, natural and quick. When the child is at school, learning languages requires greater mental commitment.

AGES 0-1: THE SENSITIVE PERIOD OF ATTACHMENT

The first year of life is dedicated to the creation of **the bond of attachment**; that primal emotional and psychological bond between parent and child essential to life and to which we are all genetically inclined. From the mother-child union arises a relationship based on interdependence, which makes the mother take care of the primary needs of her baby, thereby guaranteeing their survival.

The child first explores and knows the world through the mother's body and mind. During this phase, the affective proximity and constant presence of the adult, both physical and mental, are the most important needs that the child wants satisfied. It is therefore normal for the child to make constant requests for proximity and care, to protest when the parent walks away, to have difficulty facing certain critical moments such as sleep or the discovery of food or the presence of strangers on their own. During this stage, it is good to support these needs whenever the child expresses them, in order to pass on to them the security of the attachment.

0-6 YEARS: THE SENSITIVE PERIOD OF ORDER

How many times we have noticed that children are creatures of habit, who need routine and predictable behavioral sequences! Maria Montessori called this need "the search for order", namely the need to give a logical meaning to events and assign a place and function to each thing. For a child an orderly environment means having points of reference: knowing where their favorite objects are, what function everything serves, the exact sequence of a certain behavior - such as putting the shoes on before leaving the house or always finding the

cutlery for eating in the same drawer, etc. Making the environment and our actions clear, orderly and predictable gives the child a sense of confidence, helping them perceive the world as a pleasant, predictable place, in which they can move in total tranquillity.

FROM 6 MONTHS TO 6 YEARS OF AGE: THE SENSITIVE PERIOD OF MOVEMENT

Maria Montessori dedicated several chapters to the importance of movement. Muscles are a system of relation, because they put a person in relation with the world and other people. For this reason, the child will have a strong need to make increasingly subtle and complex movements because these will allow them to interact with their surroundings. From 6 months on, once the child is able to sit and thus adopt a different perspective of the reality around them, they will be driven by a strong push towards the environs, which translates into the need to touch everything that they see, pick up whatever falls into their peri-personal

space, use every means to reach interesting objects placed at a distance, and consequently learn to roll, then to drag themlsevs, then to crawl, and finally to walk. Once there, they will need to move through space with ever greater awareness and in a more complex manner, by running and climbing. Even subtle movements will become more and more interesting, as the child will express the need to unscrew caps, string beads, pick up small objects with pincers, tie laces and pull zippers, sew, cut with scissors and so on. Each time they will find immense satisfaction for the movement they managed to complete. For this reason it is important not to hinder the expression of these movements – within the bounds of physical safety – and to offer the child space and materials with which they can test those moves out in full freedom.

AGE 0-7: THE SENSITIVE PERIOD OF LANGUAGE

Language is of great value for the child's development as it is the basis of social life. Within the first months of their life, a child is already attracted to the movements of a speaking mouth and adores voices, which they soon learn to distinguish. The path to language acquisition is slow and gradual and follows the natural rhythm of each child's growth. However the attraction to language exists in all children, regardless of the speed with which they learn to speak it. For this reason, it is useful to provide incentives – even in several languages at the same time – by reading, telling stories and through frequent dialogic interaction. After the age of 3, developmental tools are also important, i.e. materials that allow the child to work specifically on the alphabet and their language knowledge.

AGE 0-6: THE SENSITIVE PERIOD OF THE SENSES

Sensorial education begins at birth because the child apprehends through their body. If sight is initially the sense that is the most stimulating and in greatest need of stimulation, followed by touch and hearing, at around the age of 2 we can observe an increase in the child's interest in all sensorial experiences:

The child is being curious about new flavors and attracted to objects, wanting to feel their texture and register tactile differences. The child also enjoys smelling aromatic plants or spicy food, actively looks for music and shows a spontaneous interest in rhythm and melody. Within this period, an immense variety of materials and activities can be offered to the child in order to promote their own particular sensitivity to sensorial experiences.

AGE 18 MONTHS-7 YEARS: THE SENSITIVE PERIOD OF SMALL OBJECTS

It is common to see children of about 18 months of age being fascinated by miniscule objects, which they try to seize with their expert little fingers, holding them with difficulty but feeling great joy at being able to keep them in their hands or put them into bowls or boxes. The development of the eye-to-hand coordination happens in this period, which is why the child chooses activities to test themselves on this front. We can offer various materials to the child to facilitate their need to manipulate small objects, for example the activity of pouring pasta pieces, buttons, peas, beans, bread crumbs or anything else that can be grasped between their tiny fingertips.

AGE 0-6: THE SENSITIVE PERIOD OF SOCIAL LIFE

When reaching around 2 years of age, the child appears particularly sensitive to the idea of belonging to a social group with rules of coexistence. This is therefore the best moment to learn the so-called good manners: how to thank, apologize, ask for permission, respect others' toys, wait for one's turn during a game in the park and so on.

Raising Our Children
with the Montessori Method

Reflections on the method

"The fundamental concept in education is to not become an obstacle to the development of the child. Knowing what to do is not fundamental nor difficult; what is crucial is figuring out which presumptions, which stupid prejudices we must shed off in order to make ourselves qualified to educate the child."

As we have seen, Montessori's pedagogy is based on precise theoretical concepts, which have been tested and studied ever since Montessori's direct experience with children in her schools. We have no doubts about the method's effectiveness and success within the scholastic environment; Montessori schools are becoming ever more widespread throughout the world.

But how can we as parents take advantage of the Montessori principles? Is it possible to apply this method to a domestic setting as well? Is giving the child the materials designed by Montessori enough to provide a Montessori education? Is it a costly method that is not accessible to everyone? What are the elements essential to an education that adhere to the Montessori approach?

Let's try and confront these qualms together and come up with useful answers.

For some people, the Montessori philosophy may seem very simple to follow; for others, highly complex. It basically depends on our initial interpretation of the child and on our willingness to integrate or modify our point of view.

If we are used to regarding the child as a baby created to resemble us and we firmly believe in the educational power of obedience, then we will certainly have a somewhat tough time adopting the Montessori approach. If, on the other hand, we are naturally inclined to see the child as an autonomous being who requires attention and stimulation, but not malleable, then we are already ahead of the game. One thing is certain: we must not radically alter our way of being a parent for our child. The starting point is to become aware of how we act, think and respond to their needs, and then to integrate the principal elements of the Montessori education as well as its materials and its activities into our way of parenting and our everyday life.

If we feel that we need strategies for managing certain aspects of our educational style, or simply wish to assure ourselves that we are giving our child the right stimuli and guiding them in the right direction, then there are many useful ideas for opening the doors of our home to the Montessori method.

Here are the principal elements.

First of all the method is an approach based on the **respect** for the child, their nature, their phases and their needs; an approach that encourages **the spontaneous emerging** of the capabilities that the child is naturally equipped with. Great emphasis is placed on the use of the five senses, which are believed to be closely related to the child's cognitive development. What is essential is to make the child an **active subject** and a participant in the choices made during the educational process as this makes them more independent. It is important that the **educational stimuli** be **enjoyable, engaging** and **aesthetically pleasing**, because the learning coming from the pleasure of doing such an activity is more natural and long-lasting. Montessori believed that giving external rewards or compensations to motivate a behavior or an activity serves no purpose. The implicit pleasure of carrying out an action, the satisfaction of having completed it autonomously, and the power to recognize a mistake by themselves are the elements that make a child's activity effective and self-regulated. A central role in the learning process is played by the environment, which must be simple, clean, aesthetically pleasing, orderly, well organized and pre-arranged to comply with the stages of the child's growth.

Finally, adults play a fundamental role. Montessori defines them as **prepared adults**. They play the role of **guide** and **model** for the child and are not a point of authoritarian reference; the child can imitate a particular form of behavior because they see the same behavior in the parent, not because they fear them.

The Montessori method therefore pays special attention to all that belongs to the inner world of the child, to their mind and also to their spirit. But it also cherishes the adult, who is reminded that **every parent is the best possible parent for their child.**

THE THREE PILLARS OF THE MONTESSORIAN EDUCATION

"The first duty of an educator is to stimulate life and leave it free to develop. For such a delicate mission, one needs to master the great art of suggesting the right moment, of limiting intervention, disturbance or deflection. It's the art of simply helping the soul that comes to life and that will live by virtue of its own efforts."

The Montessori pedagogy establishes 3 fundamental pillars that constitute the context of the child's life and are at the base of the educational project: the prepared adult, the prepared environment and the materials.

The base of the pyramid is the **prepared adult**. What does this mean? The Montessorian parent is an adult who confidently welcomes the vital impulse of their child; a parent who has rid themselves of fears, prejudices and preconceptions about their own behavior and is therefore conscious, respectful, confi-

dent, and sufficiently prepared about the principles of the Montessori method.

So, let us begin with self-awareness. Before dismantling the home and running to buy Montessori-style materials and reduced-scale furniture, or else subjecting the child to coloring endless tables with finger paint or tracing letters in the flour, let's pause for a moment to reflect on a few questions.

What are my thoughts on education? How confident am I in the child's abilities, and how indispensable do I feel to each of their actions? How much do I intervene in their games? How do I usually suggest them?

Good, we've taken the first step towards the Montessori method. Now let's move on to some practical suggestions.

THE PREPARED ADULT

"The adult sticks to their duty as a leader and guide; they are only an aide, a servant, as the in-

fant's personality develops through its own strength, by carrying out its activities." Being a Montessori parent may seem complex but actually, Montessori suggests the simplest, perhaps too often forgotten, thing: to follow nature and instinct. Amongst the primary needs of a child is also the feeling of being in a relationship, in a safe place, where they feel protected, listened to and understood. We thus discover that objects, even less the expensive ones, are not fundamental. Equipment does not occupy the first place. What is fundamental is our attentive gaze, our reassuring embrace, our active listening, our careful words and even our respectful silence. What we need is a sense of trust towards the child's abilities, patience towards their spontaneous actions and an acceptance of their interests, which vary throughout the different sensitive periods.

Perhaps one of the most difficult things for any parent is that of letting the child be **the master of their learning**, i.e. observing what occurs spontaneously in their daily life.

Let's look at a few examples. Faced with a new object placed on a high shelf, the child will stand on tiptoe with their arms stretching upwards to grasp it. When seeing this, our instinct may be to grasp the object for them. By waiting and observing the child's behavior, however, we may be able to discover the means through which the child prepares themselves to reach their goal: by pulling out a chair, trying to jump, using another object to reach the first one or even coming to us asking for our help. By respecting their moments of victory – always within the bounds of security and safety – we can let the child experience the immense joy that comes from the sense of self-sufficiency: "I did it!" they will be able to say or think, thus laying a new brick in the build-up of their

self-esteem. When we see that the child is using an object for a purpose other than that for which it was made, or when they don't succeed at inserting something into a designated slot, we are easily consumed by the impulse to correct it and to do it ourselves. The eagerness to straighten out something that is crooked or to intervene in a difficult situation and resolve it quickly, is the enemy of education. It's essential that we realize that these are the situations which offer unmissable educational opportunities.

The Montessori method urges us to allow ourselves to be surprised, to not expect precise behaviors from the child, but rather to let their initiative come spontaneously as a marvelous surprise, letting us be infused by a sense of wonder as we witness an act of learning.

Here's a little guide to the Montessori educational strategies that can help us to better assist our child.

1. GRANTING FREEDOM

a) of movement. "Movement is essential to life, and education cannot be viewed as a controller or, even worse, an inhibitor of movement, but solely as

an aid to expending energies well, and letting them develop normally." According to Maria Montessori, learning cannot exist without movement.

Therefore let the child lift the 2-liter water bottle by themselves, concentrate on threading a string through a hole, climb up on a pile of pillows or on wooden pegs fixed to the wall. Let them perform autonomous movements that entail muscular effort in their arms and legs.

b). of choice. "Children who can conquer themselves can also conquer freedom, as they no longer display many of those disorderly and unconscious responses that generally put children under the constant and rigid control of the adult." First of all, let's clarify a misinterpretation: freedom of choice does not mean "doing what one wants," but rather "wanting what one does." It is a matter of granting the child the possibility of exercising, thus reinforcing, their will since their earliest years; this will make the child confident and proactive because used to making autonomous choices and relying on their own ideas and inclinations as initial guide for their behavior.

c). to act. "One who is served instead of being helped, has their independence somewhat vilified." Let's allow the child the opportunity to "do it on their own," that is to win their autonomy – according to age and abilities – through their strength and mistakes.

d). to be. "It's the adult who causes the child's incapacity, confusion or rebellion; it's the adult who breaks the character of the child and represses their vital impulses. And afterwards it's the adult themselves who struggles to correct the errors, the psychic deviations, the lapses in character that they themselves have generated in the child." If we consider the child as an individual with their own legitimate and valuable ideas, desires, preferences and needs, then it will be easier for us to stay in tune with them, to ponder their behavior and place ourselves in their shoes. Even when confronted by their so-called tantrums, let's always ask ourselves: Why am I behaving in this way? How would I feel in their place? These questions will help us offer more empathetic responses and limit the child's remonstrations, as they will feel better understood.

What ingredient is indispensable to adopting this attitude? Patience. The more we succeed in being patient, the better we can succeed at accompanying our child in their growth, especially in the earliest years of life when the child is a tiny explorer, hungry for knowledge of the world around them. Since their little hands and mouth are ports of access to the world, they want to touch everything, to taste everything, and little by little, they need to ask questions and resolve a thousand "whys" in order to satisfy their hunger for knowledge. By trying to accommodate and follow these needs, we are able to fulfill them and avoid constant requests to remain unsatisfied. Furthermore, giving the child the message that what they desire is important to us, that it makes us interested in what they feel and that they can express themselves in a free context - within defined limits - helps the child attribute value to themselves and trains them to listen to and trust their own feelings.

Our undeniable effort is rewarded by the reassurance that we are equipping our little person with self-esteem and a sense of personal value, which are both basic resources for facing life with confidence.

2. RESPECT MOMENTS OF CONCENTRATION

"Little children have demonstrated the ability to work tirelessly for a long time, to focus in such a way as to disengage themselves from the outside world, revealing the constructive developments of their personality." According to Montessori, concentration is the necessary condition for the development of learning and also has a "therapeutic" effect: the child who concentrates experiences a calm and relaxing moment.

3. ACCEPT THEIR MISTAKES, TEACHING BY EXAMPLE NOT BY CORRECTIONS.

"Since the child is highly sensitive – even more than we think – to external influences, we must be very cautious in our relations with them." Let's admit that this is very difficult; the simplest response to a mistake is to say "No! Not like that!" But if we manage to suspend judgment and view the mistake as a useful attempt, not as something to be avoided but

as a starting point, then we can turn the mistake into a constructive experience. "Let's try again together," we could say, and then show the correct way to proceed, calmly and slowly, so that the child can attentively grasp every aspect of the process.

The way in which we relate to the child's mistakes will determine the relationship they will create between an error and their own sense of self-efficacy. Mr. Mistake, as Montessori called him, is a friend; rather than demonizing him, we should convey the message that he is part of life and that beneath his false disguise as an enemy, he is an ally who wishes to help us grow and improve ourselves.

4. PREPARE THE ENVIRONMENT ACCORDING TO THE CHILD'S DEVELOPMENTAL NEEDS.

THE PREPARED ENVIRONMENT

"Every child who knows how to take care of themselves, who knows how to put on shoes, how to dress and undress on their own, is the mirror of human dignity, with their joy and happiness; because human dignity comes from the sense of independence."

In the Children's Houses Maria Montessori had theopportunity to observe how children worked far more diligently and got far more involved in activities within an appropriate environment. On the other hand, she noted that there is too much distance between children and their everyday environment, which is geared to the needs of adults and thus prevents children *"from developing all their faculties in a normal manner."*

To promote the child's autonomy inside the home, it is necessary to **adapt the furniture, the types of objects as well as their quantity** to the level of our little explorer's development.

Here are the general features of a child's prepared environment.

The child 's home must above all be furnished in such a way as to guarantee the safety of the child as they move in an autonomous and independent way. The child must be free to move through the rooms and test actions autonomously. Every hazardous element must be therefore removed. Let's look at a practical example: each morning the personal hygiene routine is presented to the child. As they acquire motor skills, it is important for the child to be progressively able to try and wash their face, brush their teeth and change their clothes on their own. However, the sink most probably will not be at their height, at least at the beginning; we can set up a stool to help the child reach the tap, the child will be happy to wash themselves.

If we then hang a small towel at their height, the child can dry themselves and remember to associate the two actions in order (first to wash, then to dry).

Of course, it is recommended to place on the sink only those objects that the child can touch without danger, and for this reason it is best to keep razors, glass bottles, tiny jars, make-up and so on elsewhere.

The environment where a child lives must be orderly, pleasant to look at and comfortable to live in.

By being sure to find the objects always in the same place, the child will begin to give meaning to their surroundings. Objects acquire value because they have a place and a function, and the child will soon develop the ability to classify the objects, which is useful to their understanding of the world.

Furthermore, the presence of order in external surroundings helps with the creation of an internal order, of an orderly mind that acts according to clear and disciplined criteria and that is able to create links and associations between bits of stored information. In an orderly environment, the child creates mental frameworks that orient their feelings and perceptions, by constructing points of reference and making their surroundings predictable and comprehensible. This, however, is not a rigid and crippling order, on the contrary and by necessity it is a pleasant order, a systemization of the environment and of the objects that make it nice, pleasing to the eye and reassuring.

An orderly environment, in which every object occupies a precise place, is reassuring to the child and nurtures in them a need for order that drives the child to participate in the reorganization of objects and rooms spontaneously and on their own.

Overall, if the child can move around the house freely and autonomously, use their objects whenever they want and access them without help, then the child will feel like an active player within the household; they will feel as an integral part of the environment and will be more inspired to take care of their objects and rearrange them in such a way that they can be sure to find them again.

Let's not forget that it is essential that we build a model for the child: we are the ones to show the child how to treat objects with care, how to put them back in their place after use, how sorry we are when they break or get damaged. The example we set will be a good guide for the child.

The concept of order is also closely linked to that of **cleanliness**. It is useful to always try to leave objects clean or to place only clean ones within the child's reach so that they don't touch dirty ones. Let's show them how to clean objects from cutlery to paint brushes after each use so that they can enjoy the pleasure of being surrounded by clean objects. Montessori also suggested using light-colored, washable furniture, because it allows the child to easily detect stains, notice dirt and take action to eliminate it, thus associating the action of cleaning with the restoration of their furniture's beauty. To this end it is

useful to provide children with nice little rags, with which to dust or wash shelves. The child can thus take responsibility for the cleanliness of their surroundings. In order for the environment to be tidy, it shouldn't be too full of objects. It's therefore necessary to exercise control over the **quantity** of objects made available to the child; all materials hold greater value if they are presented as unique, since it is easier to build an association between such objects, their function, and their locations within the home.

There is no need for four different types of balls; one is sufficient to satisfy the desire to play. Different types of glasses are not necessary; two will certainly suffice. There's no need to have ten types of books available; three or four may be just as good, as long as they differ in style and content. We can keep extra

objects in a closet and offer them to the child by periodically swapping them with the ones they have.

A CHILD-FRIENDLY HOME

"It appears that due to the difference in size between the child and the objects surrounding them, the child does not know how to establish a relationship with these objects and consequently, cannot achieve their natural development."

Preparing the environment to meet the child's developmental needs requires careful observation of the surroundings, a fair amount of imagination and the ability to ask ourselves what might serve, attract, or harm us if we were a child of the same age as our son or daughter.

Let's begin by observing the spaces in our home: sit down on the floor and adopt the toddler's perspective of the house, observing the different rooms and understanding the advantages and shortcomings of our home so that it may be safe and accessible to the autonomous child. What features might be dangerous or risky for the child? And what tools can we offer them so that they can independently carry out certain activities (such as brushing teeth, putting on shoes, choosing toys and rearranging them) and participate more in the family's life (for example, by setting the table, washing dishes or taking out the trash)?

In Montessori's writings we can find some instructions on the furniture to choose for the environment where a child lives. She recommends, for example, that the furniture should be light enough to be easily moved even by a toddler. Moreover, because it makes an annoying noise when sliding on a surface, it can teach the child not to drag it across the floor. By being light, it can easily fall if struck and can therefore teach the child to pay attention to their movements.

Colorful and detailed paintings or photographs of family members can be displayed on the walls; it is important that they are hung at the child's eye level, so that they can observe them from up close and appreciate the features, and perhaps even ask questions about what they see. The same applies to all objects (books, toys, paints, but also clothing and cutlery) that are useful to the child and that they must be able to access independently.

Last but not least, the child must be able to use everything that they need to participate in the tidying up and the cleaning of the house, i.e. sweeping the floor, dusting, removing a stain etc. In the Montessori approach, it is important that even cleaning items are aesthetically pleasing as beauty invites activity and work. According to Montessori, there is a *mathematical relationship between the beauty of the environment and the emotivity of the child.* If for example, the child has to use a broom to sweep the floor, they will certainly do so more willingly if the broom is pretty rather than an old, ugly one.

The furniture too must be aesthetically pleasing; that's why Montessori suggests that it be made of washable materials or covered with slipcovers and upholstery that can be thrown into the washing machine.

Some of the objects and furniture typically used in the Montessori approach to stimulate the child inside the house are commercially available. What distinguishes this so-called Montessori furniture from standard home furniture is the fact that it is designed specifically to meet the needs of a child, not those of an adult. It obviously has smaller dimensions and more safety features. Here are some suggested measures to adopt in each room.

THE KITCHEN

The kitchen is the room where we tend to spend most of the time during the day, as it is the place where we cook, we often eat and sometimes even work. Our presence in the kitchen may make this room of great interest for the child, who will want to explore its every corner and participate in the activities that occupy us for long stretches of time. Certain precautions can therefore turn useful.

In the kitchen the child can have their own set of eating utensils that are adapted to the motor and cognitive skills of their age: a tiny dish, a glass with handles, tiny cutlery, a rounded knife and so on. What really makes a difference is that these tools be placed in a drawer that is accessible to the child, i.e. at their height and away from dangerous objects (sharp knives, heavy pots etc.); this way the child can set their place to eat, get a glass to drink when they are thirsty or a dish when they want a snack. Maria Montessori felt that it was important that children have real dishes – therefore even drinking cups made out of glass – from an early age. The act of handling them and seeing them shatter if they fall heightens the child's awareness and gives them greater control over their movements, so they may avoid repeating the experience.

A mistake is always the best form of learning. We can place all the food that we deem healthy for the child or that we want them to eat during the day on a shelf at their height. It is important to select the food (type and quantity) that we decide to make accessible to the child, so that we don't have to forbid the child from touching it nor stop them from eating too much; on the contrary, we should encourage the child to have autonomous access to food and heed their own appetite. For example, we can make them find a box of cookies with the amount that we allow them to eat throughout the day. We can vary the food, giving them cookies one day, bread or fruit on another. In this way we retain control of the child's diet but grant them the autonomy to eat on their own.

The child's curiosity finds ample space for expression within the kitchen. Drawers, cupboards, shelves and doors are fascinating and incentivize exploration. Let's help the child follow their instinct and organize the kitchen shelves in such a way that they have safe objects at their heght.

Keep available medium-sized pots, wooden spoons, cutlery (if we don't want to leave out the ones we use on a daily basis so that we do not have to continuously wash them, we can put them on high shelves and keep on hand some other cutlery or buy some wooden/hard plastic cutlery solely for the child), plastic canisters of all sizes, caps of various sizes and material etc.

We can also leave fruits and vegetables with thick skin - such as oranges, potatoes and carrots - or jars with variously shaped pasta which the child can han-

dle or play with by pouring it in and out of pots. The child will be happy experimenting with various tactile and visual sensations, placing jars inside each other, transferring objects, trying to stacks pots and noticing by themselves when things don't fit into one another. Once the child gets older, we can also provide them with larger, heavier containers: a potato peeler, a wooden chopping board, a rolling pin, cookie cutters and ingredients to bake goods, or else fruit and vegetables to peel and cut; this way we gradually make the child participate more fully in the daily life in the kitchen and involve them even in the preparation of meals.

One of the child's greatest needs is to reach our height; this way they can observe our movements and the sequence of our actions with great attention, learn from our example and personally participate in

some activities. It can be quite helpful to keep a large and stable stool or ladder in the kitchen, where the child can climb on and reach the height of the table, of the sink or of any other work surface we use. High stools, known as learning towers, can be easily found on the market; they are useful tools that children like very much. Another series of objects that the child appreciates are cleaning tools: brooms, rags and sponges fascinate toddlers.

Let's therefore prepare a drawer – the lowest one – with colored rags (like scraps of old bedsheets, pieces of old sweaters or torn blankets), sponges of various materials, towels and clothes pegs. The child will be happy to take part in the house-cleaning and to deal autonomously with minor accidents, such as spilt water, dropped food or crumbs scattered on a chair.

THE LIVING ROOM

The living room is often the room with elegant, costly and delicate furniture. It is also the room where we meet to converse and share our free time, the little ones included. It's not easy to reconcile these two qualities of the living room while integrating the needs of young children. It demands some foresight. Chinaware and glassware, ceramic trinkets, crystal tables, Chinese vases and all the costly things that we put on display here are very attractive to the child, but also quite dangerous.

By adhering to the Montessorian principle of respect for the child's freedom, it is therefore good to organize the furniture in such a way that precious objects are inaccessible and to place at the child's height other interesting objects that are suitable for them. In this way, the child can move freely through the living room and participate in our moments of recreation.

It may be useful to create an area entirely dedicated to the child within the living room. For example, one may consider offering them a colorful rug entirely for themselves along with a small, open low shelf, on which toys, books, paints and construction blocks can be placed. We can also place an armchair or a small sofa there, possibly covered with a cloth, which can serve as a wonderful gym for the child to test their ability to climb, roll and jump.

We can also organize a small bookcase, again at the child's height, or dedicate the lowest shelf of our bookcase to accommodate the child's books, perhaps coming up with types of books that differ from those in their bedroom: for example, fairy tales and stories that we can read to them, or photography books that we can browse together. In this way, the child will be able to access the books whenever they want to and maybe imitate our healthy habits, such as that of sitting in an armchair to read or sharing a few pages before going to bed.

Another entertaining activity that we can reserve for the living room is playing with music. Electronic devices - the sound system, the television, the iPod connected to the speakers - are usually all kept in the living room. We can allow the child to select music to listen to and we can get involved in their dancing and singing.

We can try playing melodies together and following a rhythm with simple instruments. We can gather sound-making objects in a basket: rattles, various tambourines, whistles, bells, castanets, oriental music instruments or items that make a noise, such as a tin box or stainless steel teaspoons. In accordance with the Montessori principle of order and peacefulness, it

is better not to superimpose music or have background noise coming from a turned-on television or radio while the child is focused on playing with something else. In situations like this, music would overtake the child's game and interfere with their concentration. Let's remember to propose one activity at a time; it is good to appreciate music when it is all about singing and moving to the rhythm, and silence when it comes to other games that require concentration.

And television? It's impossible to ignore this now indispensable and ubiquitous home appliance. We are all aware of its risks and its potential harm; however, we find it difficult to renounce this form of emotional hyper-stimulation, because it offers such a quick, easy and effective remedy for boredom and frees us from the problem of filling up our free time with other activities.

By the same token, prohibiting it would be pointless as it is part of our world. What the Montessori approach might suggest is to place this device at the service of the child's development too and its use regulated. We can set rules for watching TV: it should not be used as a background for other activities; it should only be turned on for specific programs, at the end of which it should be switched off; programs should be selected according to features that must be age-appropriate for the child, and for the most part we should try and watch programs together in order to prevent television from leading to isolation.

It can therefore become a useful instrument for heightening awareness, practicing sustained attention and sharing opinions and emotions. The same principles can be applied to the computer, the tablet, the mobile phone and all the electronic devices that fill the homes of younger generations.

THE BEDROOM

The child's bedroom is the perfect realm for their activities. It's their lab, where day after day they feel free to express their need to move, experiment with their senses, build and destroy objects and put their skills to the test. But it's also the place where the child can retreat to rest and satisfy their need for sleep. We therefore need several pieces of strategic furniture.

Naturally there should be no lack of low shelves on which games and toys can be placed, so that the child can pull them off and put them back on after use. It's enough to leave out only one game of each type (for example, a toy with pegs and slots, a jigsaw, a set of construction blocks, a box of toy figures etc.) and keep the rest elsewhere, swapping them periodically so that the child may be stimulated by new objects without the need to constantly buy more of them. We may negotiate that for each new toy an old one be discarded so as to avoid the accumulation of those toys that the child is no longer interested in. Materials should be divided into sectors; for example, by organizing the learning activities, the models for make-believe games, the creative materials, the coloring tools etc. into shelves, baskets, boxes and so on.

It is important that they always be in good condition and that we dispose of those broken objects that are no longer suitable for playing.

Part of the shelves must be also dedicated to books. We can choose to buy a small bookcase, the same height as the child, where we can place their activity books, sensory-stimulating books, coloring books or bedtime stories.

We can even think of including a photo album where to collect photos of significant moments and important family members.

Simple magazines or catalogs, where the child

can find countless images of objects and expand their vocabulary, are likewise useful. The child will spend pleasant moments leafing through their albums, asking for the names of new objects and repeating the names of the ones they have learned.

Most of the child's playing will take place on the floor. It's therefore useful to always cover the floor with a rug or sheet to play on, as this will set the borders of the area where the child can scatter their toys.

Some forms of play, on the other hand, require a work surface, and for this reason we may also consider finding space for a table and chair of a height suitable to the child's age: the chair should be about the height of the child's leg and the table the height of their chest when seated.

If instead the child is interested in painting, we may consider reserving a space for painting on the wall; for example, by taping up some wrapping paper on which the child can paint and draw without damaging the wall.

The bedroom is also the room where clothes are taken off. The child should have the possibility of clearly seeing their clothes at their own height so that they may choose what to wear and be able to put back what they have worn. The wardrobe should therefore be at a reasonable height, with doors that are not too high and heavy so that the child can easily open them. The rack for hanging clothes should be roughly at shoulder height. It is useful to organize clothes according to season – perhaps using labels or cardboard to keep them separate – in order to help the child associate clothes with weather. In addition, we can include a chest or a set of drawers for holding smaller items, divided by type. Each drawer should be dedicated to an article of clothing: socks and underwear, sweaters, pants, sweatshirts and so on.

It might be useful to stick a nice label on each drawer (that can easily be created with the child) depicting the piece of clothing it contains so that the child can easily remember the function of each one.

Finally, there obviously must be a bed. According to Montessori, the child must have independent access to their bed to comply with their need for rest. For this reason, the height of the bed must be minimal; a mattress on the floor would do just as great. The child should also not be enclosed inside a barred cage precisely because they must have the freedom to hop on and off the bed as they desire.

If the bed is to be free of bars, it's safer for it to be very low; different models can be found on the market, some of them include only the structure of a bed in wood, while others come with a structure resembling a house standing over the mattress.

THE BATHROOM

The bathroom is the place where water is and therefore exerts great charm on our children. Turning taps on and off is a highly amusing activity for them, especially when they succeed in producing jets and spurts of water that reach every corner of the floor. Empty shampoo and shower-gel containers become objects to fill and empty over and over, and caps can be transformed into small boats that float in the sink or in the bidet. Sponges, on the other hand, are great for practicing squeezing and creating a shower. We can decide with our child to devote some household objects to water games and organize them in a box or basket inside the bathroom cabinet.

The bathroom is also the space used for all those practices related to personal hygiene, which the child will be attracted to if we give them a chance to experiment on their own from an early age. In this respect we can use tiny bars of soap that fit into their little hands, two towels of different colors hanging at their height so that they can distinguish between the one used for hands and face and the other one for intimate hygiene. Generally speaking, it is good to dedicate a space to the child's things - such as their toothbrush, their creams and even their diapers - which they can reach on their own when necessary, thereby collaborating with the parents in their own personal hygiene routine. Ideally we should give the child the possibility to access the sink by themselves, and for this purpose we can also use the learning tower, as we do in the kitchen. If possible, on the other hand, it may be far more comfortable for the little one to have a low cabinet on which a tiny sink can be mounted or a wash basin filled with water be placed, a mirror put up at their height, items for washing hands and face, a hairbrush and some spare towels can be nicely tucked away on shelves. This small station gives the child the opportunity to wash themselves daily and perfect their abilities.

Personal hygiene practices are easily learned by imitating adults so it's easy to believe that the little one wants to have objects that recall the parent's habits: perfumes, make-up, shaving brush and razor, hair clips etc. In this case too we can retrieve objects - perfume samples, used-up cosmetics or an old brush and razor without the blade - to place within their reach and storing them in a box on a shelf.

It's useful to place a potty in the bathroom for when the younger ones are about 2 years of age (every parent can determine the best moment for their child), so that they may poop and pee inside it and become aware of what they produce – a crucial step towards achieving sphincter and bladder control. The child generally tends to be safer on a small potty, where they can sit on and get up from on their own, rather than on a flushing toilet, where the child is suspended above the ground and placed on top of a large hole, from which they cannot get off without an adult's assistance.

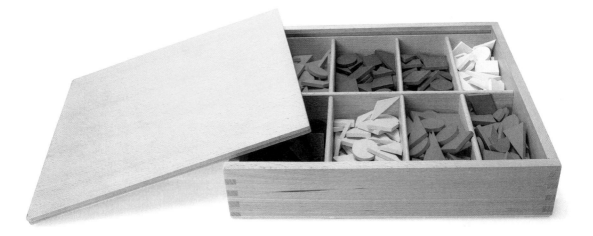

THE PREPARED MATERIALS

"Through the exploration of the environment, intelligence builds a wealth of operative ideas, without which its abstract operation would lack foundation, precision, accuracy and inspiration. This contact is established through the senses and through movement."

To complete the Montessorian education we obviously need the materials to organize the child's activities, so that the child is allowed to develop their abilities thanks to the lesson that comes from concrete experience.

Maria Montessori observed that the children's knowledge of the world develops from an innate instinct, an impulse towards a purposeful action - which she calls "the internal teacher" - that manifests itself through practical experience. The adult's task is to offer the child the conditions and tools they need to conduct their own autonomous education.

From her observations, she found that children had a constant need to grab objects, handle them and explore reality through their hands and senses. For this reason, she created an entire series of materials and called them developmental materials, as

they involve the child in a practical game that promotes their cognitive and emotional development through the use of sensorial exploration. *"The sensory material is a system of objects grouped according to a certain physical characteristic, such as color, shape, size, sound, texture, weight, temperature etc."*

These materials are the result of experimental studies; in other words, they are conceived and constructed in accordance with specific learning objectives and are validated through the observation of children's responses to the proposed stimuli.

These tools concretize concepts facilitating the child's understanding of them. They enable learning through action, gradually accompanying the child through the processes of abstraction. They start with the child's first sensory experiences and stand by the child during their gradual conquest of language, arithmetic and geometry, up to cultural insights into history, geography, literature and so on.

All the materials have specific characteristics.

Each material is made in such a way as **to isolate one attribute** (for example color, shape, size, sound, texture, weight etc.) as a learning object for the child.

This is achieved through making objects that are

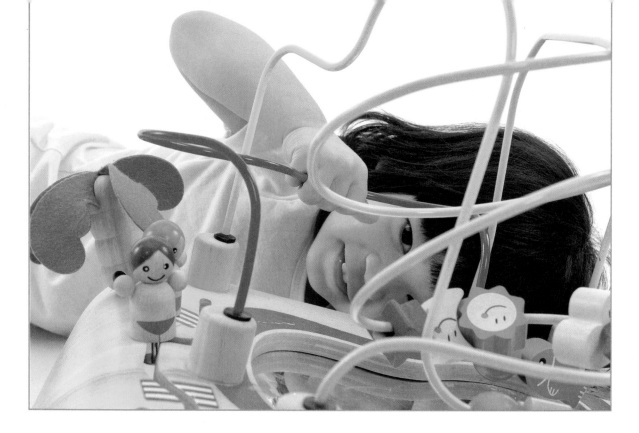

identical to one another, apart from one quality. For example, they may be forms of equal size but of different color; in this way the child's attention will be more easily drawn to color analysis, without their mind being distracted by additional information. The materials are **graduated**, meaning that each individual group of objects possesses the same quality, but to a different degree, from a "minimum" to a "maximum", so when comparing two objects they clearly show the characteristic of the material.

Another element that distinguishes Montessori materials is **the check for mistakes**. A clear example are shape sorters: in the case of solid pieces, geometric shapes must be inserted into slots that correspond to their shape. This way, any error will appear obvious: if the child tries to insert a piece that is shaped differently from the slot, they will not succeed in doing so and will be forced to look for another slot. It is thanks to this immediate feedback on their action

that the child can realize on their own whether or not they have recognized the shape and seek other operative strategies. Handling solid shapes in their little hands, the child can discover corners, lines, curves, notice differences between shapes and look for corresponding slots.

Like the environment, materials must be **attractive too**, clean and aesthetically pleasing to the eye. Wooden toys have an interesting texture, are heavier, and usually aesthetically attractive; for these reasons they are the most frequently used in the Montessori world.

The material must be able to offer the child the possibility of **performing actions**, i.e. of playing an active role. It must be a material that the child can do something with; if the child can build, modify, move, and organize the material, then it will activate their interest, lead to concentration and generate learning. The hand and the mind are closely connected: every activity must be done with the hand because the hand is guided by the mind, and the development of the mind needs the hand. We might say that young children think with their hands.

As already noted, the playing material must be in **limited** quantity. The child needs the right objects to be available at the right time. It is therefore enough to have one set of materials for each attribute to be learned (one for shapes, colors, numbers etc.) and to change it periodically, proposing a new one in place of another.

Maria Montessori suggested presenting the child with this developmental material in **three steps**:

1. PROVIDING THE CHILD WITH INFORMATION ON THE MATERIAL

For example, when introducing shapes, show a circle to the child and tell them "this is a circle", then give the shape to the child so they can explore it and repeat its name. Do the same with two other shapes, such as the square and the rectangle.

2. RECOGNIZING THE MATERIAL BY NAME

Place shapes in front of the child and ask them to pick the shape that you name – the circle, for example. If the child picks a different one, do not register the mistake, but simply provide the word for the shape they have taken, take it into your own hands, look at it then return it to the child. Take the correct shape in your hands - in this case the circle - examine it and say its name out loud it before giving it to the child, thus repeating step 1, as noted above.

This is an important step that can be repeated several times with variations; for example, by asking the child to put the shape in certain places, to pick

it up with a specific part of their body or to recognize it amongst the objects in the room. We should not proceed to the next phase until we have made sure that the child has absorbed the information on the shape.

3. RECOLLECTING MATERIAL

This time we invite the child to name the shape we take in our hands, asking them "what is this?" If they don't say the right name, we go back to step 2.

In Montessori schools, exercises related to practical life are provided in addition to developmental materials. **Practical life** activities are most attractive to a child, because they raise them to the level of an adult; they make the child feel capable of carrying out important actions and the child can immediately

see the effects, therefore boosting their own sense of autonomy.

The chores of practical life respond to the need for movement towards a **real purpose**: washing hands, getting dressed and undressed, lacing shoes, setting up, clearing away, cleaning the floor, dusting, doing the laundry, ironing, taking care of plants, preparing a snack. With these exercises children improve their coordination, their coarse and fine motor skills, their ability to plan sequential actions and maintain attention.

Let's also keep in mind that the most attractive toys for children are **real things**. When we notice the child's interest in one of our things, we tend to buy it in plastic or wooden reproduction but are disappointed when we see that the child is not as attracted to it as they are to the real object. A doll brush is not as fascinating as a real hairbrush. A plastic coffee cup is not as interesting as the ceramic cup that mom uses in the morning. The plastic apple has nothing to do with that lovely, heavy and fragrant red apple on the kitchen table.

However, a horse made out plastic or wood, which the child can touch and handle, will be more interesting than a horse depicted on a card. Especially in their early years, children will be attracted to photographs of real objects rather than to drawings that require some ability for abstraction. In general, all those popular games where children only need to press buttons and wait for the audio or visual effect to be generated, are games of little interest because they are passive. The sound that the child makes by beating a ceramic cup with a steel teaspoon or a tin box with a wooden spoon, or by shaking a bag of nuts, will be far more interesting to them than the artificial sound programmed into a toy. Sensory ma-

terials and practical activities must be proposed according to the child's interests, which vary on their age and their growth phases. As Maria Montessori used to say: *"with experience, the only material suitable for education is the one that actually interests the child and spontaneously holds their interest, because the child repeatedly chooses it."* It is therefore up to the parent's attention and experience with their child to identify what may interest them, but remember that the material must meet the needs of the child and not viceversa. This means that if we notice a lack of interest in colors, it's useless to suggest and re-suggest that activity to the child only because they are at a developmental stage when they should be interested in colors. Instead, we should pay greater attention to their signals and offer them the most suitable material at that moment, so as not to lose that window of sensitivity to other areas of

learning. One of the questions arising spontaneously as we read about the features of the Montessori materials is: are they really good for playing? In an adult's mind, play-related activities are identified primarily with distraction and leisure. Our society sees leisure as the opposite of work: work is useful and demanding; playing is pleasant but not constructive. We can therefore understand how easy it is to attribute a low value to the child's recreational activities. Maria Montessori, on the other hand, reversed this idea by regarding child play as a serious matter: the child plays and works at the same time; whilst amusing themselves, they build their personality. The child is relaxing and at the same time doing something extremely important and serious because they are creating their own personality. The answer to the question is therefore affirmative: learning materials are for playing and playing is learning.

Montessori for DIY Parents: Montessorian Materials and Activities to Do at Home

Having a selection of Montessorian materials at home is definitely a choice that can benefit the child's growth. Nonetheless you should make a preliminary consideration: are you one of those parents who has decided to enroll their child in a Montessori school? Or are you simply interested in the approach and wish to integrate it into your home environment?

In the first case, you should make sure that the school materials are not the same as those offered at home so as to avoid confusion and the possibility of differences in the way you and the teacher present them to the child. If one wishes to faithfully reproduce the Montessori school at home, there are many commercially available materials to do this; in such case, however, it would be useful to undergo more specific training in order to make a conscious and correct use of them from an educational point of view.

If, on the other hand, you simply want to make your style of educating Montessori-like by offering your child activities that evoke the Montessori method, then there is the problem of choosing games and creating activities.

CREATING MONTESSORIAN GAMES AND TOYS

Let's begin with toys that are available on the market. First of all, we can start making purchases that are more geared towards the Montessori principles, i.e. we can buy toys that meet certain criteria. We can make sure that there are not too many categories in any one game, i.e. colors, shapes and sizes are not too mixed up. The more those concepts are separated, the clearer the toy will be to the child, who will be able to use it autonomously. Let's aim for toys that allow the child **to perform actions**, that invite them to act and not

remain passive while the toy is in operation.

Construction blocks, modeling clay, shapes to cut out, puzzles to complete, musical instruments to shake and play are therefore welcome. We should prefer toys with a **clear purpose**, such as learning how to cut fruit, grab small objects, recompose puzzle shapes, link corresponding shapes or colors.

Let's create space for **musical instruments**, even simple ones, to sensitize the child to rhythm.

We need to remember that activities that require handling are fundamental; for this reason, it is important to offer concrete objects that the child can handle and encourage them to use finger paints, clay and plasticine, depending on the age.

With a young child, we prefer **concrete material**, or rather, three-dimensional material that they can touch and explore. From the age of 3, one can gradually begin combining concrete materials with two-dimensional ones, such as **photographs and drawings**.

Generally, all activities should use **real-world** materials. According to Montessori, a young child is not ready for fantasy and abstraction, so it's pointless to offer them materials with characters drawn from fantasy and the world of fairy tales; by leading into a different realm and creating a distance from reality, they can confuse the child. The child is incapable of abstracting and building an understanding of a make-believe world or justifying the fact that it does not exist. So at least during their early years, it's far more useful for their development to resort to materials from the context of real life.

To this end, we can unleash our initiative by finding materials of any kind and substance, suitable for Montessorian playing inside the home.

If we look around, there are various developmental materials in the house: kitchen utensils, sponges, rags, stationery supplies - colored crayons, scissors and glue - various kinds of food such as rice, beans, dried fruit, variously shaped pasta, flour, spices, jars and boxes of different shapes and sizes, fabrics, buttons and strings.

But what kind of playing approach makes a material in line with the Montessori approach?

1. The way to play with the child.

There are different ways to play with a child; doing so in the Montessori manner means genuinely having fun together. First of all, it means sitting next to the child as an equal and having the desire to be and do something with them in a calm and patient manner, freeing the mind from distracting thoughts and taking our time in total tranquillity. Feeling that our interest is sincere and seeing that we are having fun, brings great satisfaction to the child, because it makes them feel important and emotionally welcome. If the adult takes a strictly educational and scholastic approach, then the activity will become stiff, possibly too high-performing and therefore wearisome for the child. We must remember that the child should have fun and take pleasure in the execution of the activity. On the other hand, while amusing themselves, they are learning as well, as Montessori materials always aim at exercising a skill.

2. The material allows the child to exercise and develop skills whilst playing.

Developmental materials and practical activities always have a purpose.

3. The material should not be presented at a random moment in time, but instead suggested strategically, based on the observation of the child's interests.

4. The possibility of doing it in such a way that the child can engage in the game on their own, without the guidance and corrections of the adult.

Each material revolves around a specific quality, which the child is going to focus their attention on. It is also designed in such a way as to allow a check for mistakes, thus ensuring that the child directs their actions autonomously.

Let's take a few examples.

We may have noticed that the child repeatedly touches variously shaped objects, exploring them with their hands. We then decide to present them with some materials that deal with shapes. Let's take some simple, commercially available, wooden shape-sorting toys, or else boxes with slots of various shapes that we have made ourselves at home. We present the child with small cardboard or wooden forms, following the method of the three Montessori steps. We then suggest to the child to push them into the appropriate openings. The child can immediately tell whether or not their action is correct based on whether or not the little shape can fit through the slot.

In another situation, we observe that the child spontaneously pairs objects of the same color, for example, associates a cap with its container of the same color. We therefore propose an activity dealing with colors; we take some colored buttons, choosing no more than four distinct colors - for example, red, yellow, green and blue. Then we take some transparent caps and insert a card of the color of one of the buttons inside, so we have a cap with a blue base, one with a yellow base and so on. The child must place all the buttons inside the caps according to color, and we show them how to play. The presence of the color in the cap lets the child immediately notice if they are placing the buttons in the right cap, or if they have put one in a cap of a different color by mistake. The fact that the buttons are all the same and differ only in color, ensures the isolation of the attribute of color so the child is working solely on this category. Also, the fact that the number of buttons in each color is the same ensures that the child is working solely on the characteristic of color.

This way we have acted on several levels: we have followed the child's interest and we have given them a chance to experiment autonomously, by exercising their fine manual and problem-solving skills, whilst the child has been amusing themselves.

What if the child does not avail themselves of the mistake check?

It can happen that the child makes a mistake without realizing it, without taking advantage of the error-control strategy. This information is important,

because it's telling the adult that they are not ready to perform that specific activity. If we recall that the child has an inner teacher who guides them in their growth and develops their potential in a natural manner, such behavior makes us understand that we are suggesting an activity that does not correspond to the development stage and the interest of the child. This activity can therefore be set aside and re-proposed later on. If the child is ready to be receptive to this kind of task, they will automatically make use of the error-control strategy on their own.

But how do we know what the correct form of play to propose to the child is?

Let's go back and stress an already articulated concept: observation is the indispensable element of the Montessori educational approach. The Montessorian parent is a patient parent, one who observes, who does not interrupt, who awaits the child's movements, who gives a meaning to mistakes and is in tune with the child's evolutionary impulses, both cognitive and emotional ones. Observing the child will make us notice changes in their behavior; if we are on the street, for example, and the child begins to notice details, to point at objects and things, then they are manifesting the need to begin classifying the world and arranging it in categories. From one day to the next, the child

may start getting fascinated by animals or plants and appreciate the sounds of their names: they may display a new interest in language; or they may repeatedly go off searching for small objects, which they can grab with their hands and hold between their fingers, or again they may try to unscrew corks and open hinges: they are telling us that they may need fine motor activities. We may notice that the child immediately grows bored before a box of colors, while spending a great deal of time trying to climb on the sofa, rolling on the floor or sitting on a chair: they are expressing a need for movement and corporeal experience. Alternatively we may see them spending time filling and emptying containers: they are practicing the concept of empty/full.

From the cues that we gather by observing the child's gestures, we can understand what kind of activity they may need, and we can then prepare for it with what we have at home or by purchasing specific items.

These stimuli can then be accepted or not by the child; the adult proposes the activity, showing them

how it's done and waits for a response. If we see them focused on the activity, then it is suitable for the child, who feels satisfaction in the effort and has fun repeating it several times. Whenever the child discovers an activity that corresponds to their sensitive learning window, they will want to repeat it over and over for a variable period of time. This is the phase in which new brain connections are created and reinforced, so repetition must be welcomed and encouraged.

If the child shows interest, then the adult will have to continue, even creating different activities related to the same category of learning. If, however, the child is not that attracted to a form of play, then the adult can put it aside and return to observing the child in order to get new ideas for activities to propose at this specific moment of their development. The child remains the principal guide in every Montessorian activity.

HOW TO PLAY WITH OUR CHILD

To play with a child takes patience, calm and trust.

It is advisable to leave the child free to choose playing activities, either in total freedom or – as it happens with younger children - between two options, as in "do you prefer to play with shape sorters or colors?" This allows the child to accomplish the action of choosing and listening to their inclinations and desires.

We can present them with developmental materials by following the three steps of the Montessori method and then wait for their response; or, if it's a case of creative play or board games, we can let the child explore the material on their own and ask us for help, thus paying attention to their needs without anticipating their discoveries.

If the child makes a mistake or is struggling with

the activity, it is good to take a deep breath and learn the value of waiting. We need to think that the child is not making a mistake in the way they use the object, and is not facing a difficult moment that requires our immediate intervention (unless expressly requested). Let's not measure the time they need to reach their goal; this is not a case of wasted effort but a very useful attempt at concentration. Through their effort, the child is experiencing a great opportunity. They are activating their skills in order to engage in purposeful behavior. By the end of the process the child will have discovered a new skill. Were we to intervene, we would interrupt this process, thus preventing this discovery.

During playtime, we can talk to the child if we see them inclined to interaction and not concentrating on a solitary task. When the child speaks to us, we can stimulate dialogue with sentences that prompt them to continue with what they are saying, such as: "Really? And then what happened? Tell me. I'm listening." You can also repeat what the child has just said, demonstrating that you have listened; or you can explain and describe what the child is doing, by saying: "We are feeding the cow," or "We are looking for the slot for the circle," or "We are coloring with the yellow pencil."

The same goes for their emotions. We can verbalize for the child how they are responding to certain circumstances; if, for example, the child gets angry because they are failing at a game, we should explain to them the emotion we are seeing by saying something like: "I understand; being unable to put the circle in the slot makes you angry." - obviously avoid judging, criticizing or deprecating the emotions expressed by the child. When we see the child struggling with an activity and wanting to abandon it, our job is to encourage them, telling them that they shouldn't give up, that with more effort they will be able to do it. We must find expressions capable of reinforcing the value of commitment and effort as well as the gratification that arises from commitment.

Suggested Activities

In this section we explore the life in the Montessori laboratory. Be ready to transform your kitchen, a desk or a rug in your living room into a genuine work space for your child, where you can watch them create things, handle them, learn, concentrate, make mistakes and rejoice.

You will be direct spectators of their victories and proud observers of their growth. Don't worry, though: these are not complex activities with endless steps and many, difficult-to-find materials. Quite the opposite; most of the suggested activities make use of recycled materials and of objects that you already have at home or can easily purchase. Generally speaking, they are deliberately simple activities, accessible to everyone, quickly implemented and easily inserted into moments of everyday life. The snack time, the preparation of a lunch or a house-cleaning session can turn into precious occasions for developing abilities. Even the simplest games can end up being highly educational. What counts is the way we present them.

For each activity you will find the materials that are required, the educational objectives that it helps develop - the acquisition of practical skills, the comprehension of concepts and the development of cognitive skills - and an explanation on how to perform it. Suggestions on how to vary the activities and adapt them to different ages are also provided, so that they can be conducted at different stages of the child's growth. Keeping in with Montessori's philosophy, the activities are flexible and thus adaptable to children of various ages or at different development stage. You will therefore find only the indication of the approximate age from which to propose the activity and its difficulty level, without any restrictive measures except for those related to the child's safety.

Don't be afraid to involve your child in new sensorial experiences as these will always be a precious opportunity for them to grow and learn. The important thing is to ensure their safety, through a well-aimed choice of materials and with your reassuring presence at their side.

Older children, on the other hand, can perform their activities independently and even keep themselves busy by preparing the materials. All the suggested activities can spark the interest of children approximately up to the age of 7. You will also find directions on your parental role within the game, whether it is that of an integral and interactive participant or a simple supervisor. Set aside some time to dedicate yourself to the activities, even if they are quickly and easily performed. The positive feelings that you will share with your child during these moments will be of great help to their acquisition of new skills. Consider dedicating a precise and delimit-

ed space to each task so the child learns to understand that there are limits to their actions. In addition, remember that each activity begins with the presentation of the materials—always arranged in a clear, orderly and logical manner—and ends with the tidying up of the work surface, so the child internalizes the importance of order and of keeping their belongings clean.

Following the structure of the activities that Montessori developed for her schools, the games have been divided into 3 categories: learning through sensorial experience, the practical experiences of everyday life and outdoor activities.

The first group of activities includes 19 games, through which the child practices movements of the hand and the wrist in preparation for writing, stimulates visual and auditive recognition, and develops their sense of smell. The activities about numbers, letters and colors offer simple tools for learning these concepts, allowing to follow the Montessori method even at home.

In the second group of activities you will find ideas for teaching your child how to take care of their personal hygiene and of their clothes, and how to get them actively involved in housework, making them feel appreciated for their important role in the family life. Finally, the last part of the section is dedicated to activities conducted outdoors, with the goal of bringing the child closer to Nature, which according to Montessori, is to be considered their indispensable companion on their path to maturity.

Good luck!

LEARNING
THROUGH SENSORIAL
EXPERIENCES

Learning numbers creatively

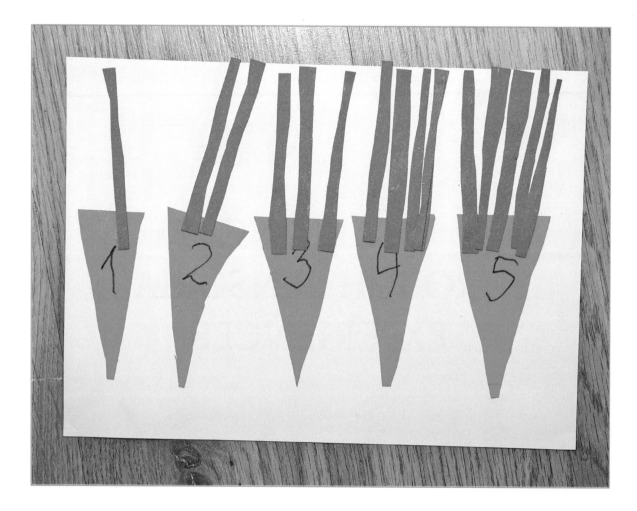

MATERIALS

ORANGE AND GREEN A3 CARDBOARD, GLUE, SCISSORS, MARKER.

OBJECTIVES - This is a simple and easy-to-do activity to get children to learn the numbers 0-9, helping them memorize through touch and a three-stage lesson.

HOW TO DO IT - The methods for introducing numbers can vary; here we propose an activity with paper carrots. On the orange cardboard draw 10 rectangular triangles with their tips pointing downwards. At the center of each triangle write a number between 0 and 9 in clear letters, or else print the numbers, cut them out and glue them on the carrots. Then cut out the carrots and lay them all down in a row from 0 to 9 on an A3-size sheet, so that the child can see the numerical sequence. Now take the green cardboard and cut out forty five 1" wide strips that are as long as the triangles.

The materials are ready. Sit with the child to your left with the series of carrot before you. Present the numerical sequence to the child. Touch the number 0 with the index and middle fingers, trace its oval shape while saying three times out loud: "how we write zero." Then repeat the action with the number 1. Now ask the child to repeat your actions, i.e. to trace the shapes of the numbers 0 and 1 with their index and middle fingers. Then ask them to point to the numbers ("touch the number 0"); finally, point to 0 , then to 1 and ask them to tell you what number it is ("what number is written like this?"). If the child learns both numbers, proceed to the next two numbers, otherwise start all over again, making them touch 0 and 1. The next task is to associate numbers with quantity. Take the green strips and paste on each carrot the number of strips that corresponds to its number.

Always touch the number with the index and middle fingers while speaking the name of the number out loud, then let the child glue the strips. Make the child note that another strip must be added to each number as the numbers proceed from 0 to 9.

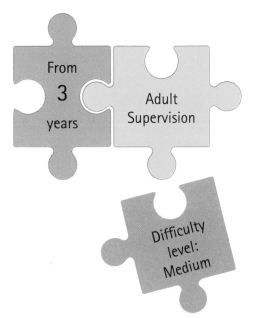

From 3 years

Adult Supervision

Difficulty level: Medium

This activity of associating quantities with numbers can be done with objects of any type.

We can print numbers on cards or write them down on a foam sheet and then cut them out, so to turn them into three-dimensional objects; this way the shape can be perceived more clearly through touch. We can prepare some containers with objects and place each of them beneath a foam number based on the quantity of objects they represent.

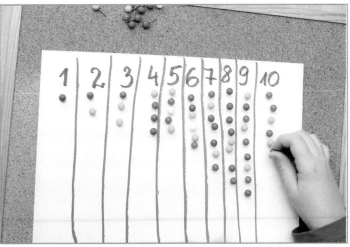

Counting quantities and associating them with numbers by using dried legumes

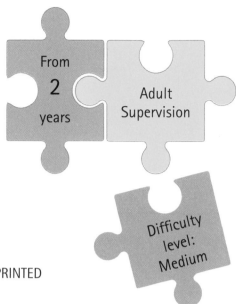

From **2** years

Adult Supervision

Difficulty level: Medium

MATERIALS
10 EMPTY JARS, A PLATE OF LEGUMES, NUMBERS FROM 0 TO 9 (PRINTED ON CARDS OR MADE OF PLASTIC/WOOD/FOAM).

OBJECTIVES - This activity trains the child to create an association between numbers and quantity and exercises their fine motor skills.

HOW TO DO IT - Arrange the numbers in front of a row of 10 jars. Then place the plate with the legumes before the child and in front of the jars. Ask the child to place as many legumes in each jar as indicated by the number before it. Start the activity by providing the child with an example; say "this is zero" while tapping the number with your index and middle fingers. Then remind the child that zero corresponds to no quantity, so we do not put any legumes in that jar. Then make them proceed on their own. If the child makes a mistake, do not correct them and let them continue to the very end.

Once the activity has been completed, check the child's work by asking them to count the legumes

in each jar and see whether the number is identical to the number before the jar.

To perform this activity the child must already have done exercises that involve numerical sequence from 0 to 9 and know how they are written.

In case of younger children, merely ask them to place the legumes in the various jars after isolating them according to type (lentils, chickpeas, beans etc.) and to count the legumes for you out loud, so that they can begin to memorize the verbal sequence as they place them in the jars.

Building sensory letters
to learn the alphabet

MATERIALS

26 LIGHT WOOD OR CARDBOARD PANELS (ABOUT 4MM THICK), SOME SQUARE SHAPED (ABOUT 5.3")
AND SOME RECTANGULAR SHAPED (FOR B, D, F, G, L, P , Q, T, Z), WITH ROUNDED CORNERS; 26 SHEETS OF
FINE SANDPAPER OR CLOTH, SCISSORS, GLUE, A CARDBOARD OR TIN BOX, A BOWL OF WATER, A TOWEL.

ORJECTIVES - This activity prepares the child to learn the letters of the alphabet, to recognize them by associating their tactile quality with their sound. The muscular memory that is involved when touching the letters facilitates the association between sign and sound.

Difficulty level: Medium

From 2 and a half years

Adult Supervision

HOW TO DO IT - First you need to prepare the sandpaper letters. They are easy to find on the market, but if you wish to build them yourself, here are some simple guidelines. Draw the letters of the alphabet on sheets of sandpaper (you can make it easier for yourself by using stencils of letters) about 4" high. Cut them out and set them aside. Then prepare the bases: ideally, you would cut them out of squared (about 5.3") and rectangled (5.3" x 3.5") plywood sheets with rounded corners, or you can look for wooden, plastic or cork coasters, or you can simply cut them out of 4mm-thick cards. Glue the sandpaper letters on the center of these cards. You can also use tactile material of a different kind, such as cloth or another other soft material. Let them dry. Get a cardboard or tin box from which you can lift them vertically. Now the materials are ready; you can present them to the child by following the three-step lesson.

Place the box of letters, the bowl of water and the towel in front of you, with the child sitting on your left. Place three randomly selected letters on the table, one next to the other. Lightly wet the index and middle fingertips of your dominant hand (so as not to soil the letters and thus make them last longer), dry them with the towel and trace the shape of the first letter. As you touch it, make the sound of the letter, for example "b", three times per letter. Ask the child to touch the letter when it's their turn, then proceed to the next letter. Then ask the child: "which letter is b?" And repeat this for all three letters. Finally, verify the child's comprehension of the three letters through repetition, by asking: "which letter is this?".

Writing and drawing
on flour and sand

MATERIALS
A TUB OR A WOODEN/PLASTIC TRAY WITH HIGH EDGES,
SAND/TABLE SALT/CORNFLOUR, CARDS WITH SANDPAPER LETTERS
(OR HAND-MADE CARDS WITH THE LETTERS WRITTEN ON THEM).

OBJECTIVES - Introduce this activity after the one with the sandpaper letters, as it helps consolidate the comprehension of the written form of the letters while exercising the movement of the wrist and the hand, thus serving as a preparation for writing; it also develops fine motor skills and concentration.

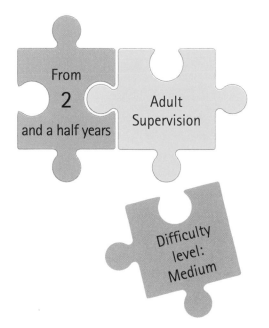

From **2** and a half years

Adult Supervision

Difficulty level: Medium

HOW TO DO IT - Place the material on a table in front of the child, who is seated on your left. Pour some sand, salt or cornflour – enough to cover the entire base – into the tub/tray. Place the first card with the sandpaper letter in front of the tub/tray (or a cardboard on which you wrote the letter, or if you don't have that, a sheet with one of the printed letters; the important thing is to present them one by one). Using your index and middle finger, touch the sandpaper letter, making the sound of the letter out loud, then reproduce it on the sand/salt/cornflour. Repeat the actions for the child and go through all the letters.

Also use the tub/tray for free-hand or copy drawing, as these are always the best activities to train the hand muscles.

Building a pink tower to learn how to compare dimensions

MATERIALS
10 WOODEN CUBES, PAINTED IN PINK AND LACQUERED, ARRANGED IN DESCENDING ORDER: THEY MEASURE 1X1X1 CM, 2X2X2, 3X3X3 ETC. UP TO THE LARGEST CUBE, WHICH MEASURES 10X10X10 CM.

OBJECTIVES - This is one of Montessori's most famous materials, used to stimulate the concept of size and organization of objects through the comparison of their dimensions, teaching the child which of multiple objects is larger or smaller; it develops fine motor skills. This is a sensory material, because it makes the child learn the characteristics of the cubes through sensory perception: in order to grab and carry them, the child must use their entire hand, opening it more as the size of the cube increases.

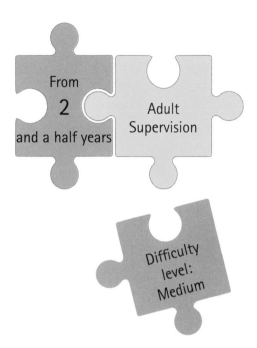

From
2
and a half years

Adult Supervision

Difficulty level: Medium

HOW TO DO IT - Get some cubes on the market or if you prefer, you can make them according to the dimensions indicated under "materials".

Place the tower of cubes, arranged one on top of the other in descending order, on a rug before the child who is seated on your left, so the child can see the final results of the activity. Then knock it down with the intention of rebuilding it together. Arrange the cubes randomly on the rug. Show the child how to carry the cubes of the tower; it is important to grab them from above, so that the child can see the variations in the opening of their hand based on the size of the cube that they are transporting.

Take the largest cube and place it in front of you; then proceed with the other cubes in order of size, until you build the entire tower. Now it's up to the child: ask them to rebuild the tower by themselves. Leave them free to touch, remove, turn the cubes and even make

mistakes when arranging them: the material already alerts the child visually about an incorrect order of the cubes, so this can serve as an independent mechanism to check mistakes. Error after error, the child will accomplish their result.

Learning colors

MATERIALS
YELLOW, RED, BLUE, GREEN, ORANGE, PURPLE, PINK, BROWN, BLACK, WHITE AND GRAY
MARKERS; 22 5X5 CARDBOARD SHEETS, SCOTCH TAPE, A BOX.

OBJECTIVES - This material takes its inspiration from Montessori Color Box number 2 and is
conceived with the goal of making the child recognize the colors and their names.

HOW TO DO IT - Take the cardboard sheets and color them – two for each color – with the
markers (if you prefer, you can use tempera paints). Make a stripe with the scotch tape along the top
and bottom of each card as if it were a small frame. Put the materials in the box, which will be used to
store the cards.

To start the activity, place the box before you and have the child on your left. Mix all the color
cards on the table. Then take the primary colors (yellow, red and blue) one at a time. For example: pick
up the red one and lay it down in front of you. Always hold the cards by the taped part, so as not to
cover the color. Then say: "now I'm looking for one like this." Look for the other red card and place it
next to the first one. Make the child notice that the colors are the same by first indicating one card,
then the other. Stick the pair of cards back in the box and proceed with the activity.

Take the yellow card and place it in front of the child. Then ask them to look for the same one.
Once the pair is made, put both cards back into the box. Proceed in this way through all the colors.

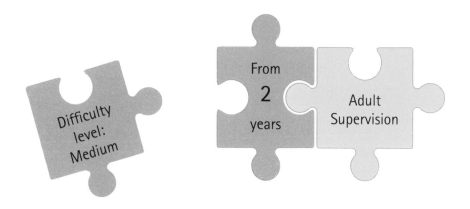

Difficulty level: Medium

From 2 years

Adult Supervision

Once you see that matching colors have been well internalized, move on and introduce the names of the colors. As you did before, arrange the materials before you and place the child on your left.

Take the red card and say, "this is red," repeating the word for the color 3 times. Then mix up the cards on the table and ask the child: "which one is red?" "can you pass me the red one?" "can you put the red one in the box?". If the child succeeds in doing so, then proceed to step 3. If not, start all over again by re-presenting the red (you don't need to draw attention to the mistake, simply start from the beginning).

In the final step, review all the cards and ask the child for the name of the color of each one. It will take some practice before the child learns the names of all the colors; in the meantime, you can make them engage in other activities (such as free-hand drawing with the colors, attaching colored clothes pegs to cards of the same color, matching cards with objects of the same color, or separating fruits and vegetables by color).

Learn the colors with fruit and vegetables

3 SMALL CONTAINERS IN YELLOW, RED AND BLUE (OR 3 COLORED PAPER CUPS), A PLATE WITH SLICES OF RED
AND YELLOW PEPPERS AND OF PURPLE LETTUCE.

OBJECTIVES - This is a classifying activity, through which the child learns colors by associating them with objects of everyday life and by performing a normal household activity.

HOW TO DO IT - You can take the opportunity to make a salad while performing this activity, using a yellow pepper, a red pepper and some purple lettuce. Present a tray with the 3 colored containers and sliced vegetables to the child. Remind the child of the word for each color by pointing at the containers (yellow, red and blue). At this point, indicate the first container and ask: "which pieces of vegetables are the same color as this red jar?" and suggest inserting the slices of vegetables in the jar.

68

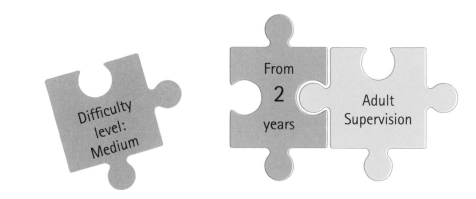

Difficulty level: Medium

From 2 years

Adult Supervision

Proceed in this way with the other colors. Another way to play with colors in the kitchen is by taking napkins in 6 colors (white, red, yellow, green, orange, blue), laying them open before the child, and asking them to go around the kitchen and hunt for fruit and vegetables and place them on the napkins of the corresponding color.

Another game can be played with freshly cut vegetables ready to be tossed in the pot of soup: say one color at a time to the child and make them select pieces of vegetables of that color, say the names of these vegetables and their color and place them in the pot. In this way, the child will learn both the colors and the words for the vegetables that go into the colorful soup.

Learning science with a home garden

MATERIALS

SOIL, SMALL POTS OR RECYCLED MATERIALS (YOGURT CONTAINERS, ROLLED-UP NEWSPAPERS, EMPTY CARDBOARD ROLLS, EGG SHELLS), PACKETS OF SEED, RAKE, TROWEL, SPOON, WATERING CAN, NOTEBOOK, CAMERA.

OBJECTIVES - Gardening activities can be done even at home with some precautions; they help learning important things about nature, the life cycle and scientific information on plants (for example, what they feed on, how they sprout etc.).

HOW TO DO IT - You can organize a box for the child where they can keep all their working tools. Together with the child you can also keep a small notebook for drawings, photographs, notes on your plants' growth, information collected from the Internet, photos showing the gradual growth

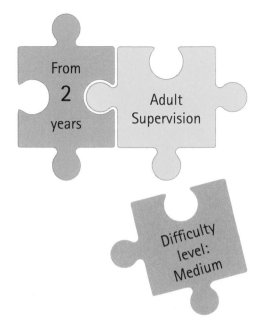

From **2** years

Adult Supervision

Difficulty level: Medium

of the plants, notes on the amount of soil you have used, the type of seeds chosen, how much you should water them, the characteristics of the leaves, the parasites from which to protect the seedling, the period of development, etc. You can start planting your small plants by getting some recycled objects, for example, empty egg shells. Ask the child to pour a bit of soil inside each shell using a spoon. Then insert a seed into the soil, first checking the depth at which it should be placed. You should choose seeds that don't take long to sprout (like beans), so that the child can learn to wait but also have the satisfaction of seeing the result of their work in a short time. Show them how to water the soil in a gentle manner, making sure not to pour the water in such a way as to disturb the soil. Do not miss your child's expression when the first shoots appear!

Creating shapes with modeling clay

MATERIALS
WAXED CLOTH, MODELING CLAY,

1 SMALL ROLLING PIN (OR A FAT MARKER),

1 PLASTIC KNIFE,

3 BOTTLE CAPS OF VARIOUS SIZES,

3 JARS OR CUPS OF VARIOUS SIZES,

2 WALNUT SHELLS, 1 CLOTHES PEG,

1 UNSHARPENED PENCIL, 1 PLASTIC FORK.

ORJECTIVES - Modeling is a highly stimulating sensory activity for a child as it involves fine motor skills, activates the muscles of the hand and the wrist and, thanks to the physical effort of kneading, stimulates concentration and creativity.

HOW TO DO IT - First, we must teach the child to work on a fixed surface, so spread the waxed cloth on a table or on the floor. Then set up all the materials on a tray, dividing them in an orderly manner: the modeling clay in a bowl (or several bowls, in case of differently colored clay), a box containing tools for cutting or indenting (plastic knife, pointless pencil), another with tools for rolling out the clay (rolling pin or thick marker) and finally all the molds suitable for the child's age that you have at your disposal (clothes peg, glasses, caps, fork, walnut shells, cookie cutters, etc.). As an activity, modeling is highly creative, so grant the child the opportunity to explore the various materials on their own: kneading, squeezing, cutting, breaking, rolling or dividing the clay into pieces – every action is welcome.

With older children, you can suggest reproducing real figures or geometric shapes, using objects as models.

Younger children, on the other hand, will probably want to divide the clay into little, confetti-like pieces rather than use the molds: let them follow their instinct; they will discover on their own that they can leave their fingerprints on the dough and from there they will begin modeling it.

From
18
months

Adult
Supervision

Difficulty
level:
Low

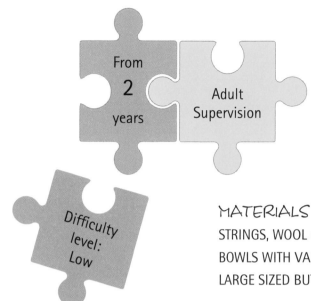

From
2
years

Adult
Supervision

Difficulty
level:
Low

Threading beads and other materials

MATERIALS

STRINGS, WOOL OR NYLON THREAD, RUBBER TUBES, PIPE-CLEANERS, BOWLS WITH VARIOUS TYPES OF PERFORATED PASTA, MEDIUM AND LARGE SIZED BUTTONS OR BEADS.

OBJECTIVES - This is a nice and enjoyable activity that develops fine motor skills, hand-to-eye coordination and concentration.

HOW TO DO IT - Arrange all the material on a tray in front of the child. Then show them how to do the activity by initiating it and explaining each one of your actions.

Choose a type of thread from those you have with you. Search amongst the objects for one with a hole of the proper size for the thread. If the thread is too thick for the hole, you will not succeed at inserting it; this obviously forces you to change the item.

Make a knot at the end of the thread, explaining to the child that this is how we avoid letting the material slip off. Take an item with the dominant hand and insert the thread into the hole with the other hand. Make the child see how the item slides down the tautly held thread until it reaches the knot.

Then, repeat the action. At this point, leave the child free to handle the material as they wish. They can continue building the necklace or start another one from scratch. They will certainly be satisfied after they have managed to insert the first item and will repeat the sequence easily and with pleasure, even alternating the various types of material.

It is advisable to leave younger children with only one type of thread – the thickest and stiffest – because it is easier to handle, and to introduce the others gradually. Watch that they do not stick small items into their mouths.

Finger painting

MATERIALS
PIECES OF CARDBOARD, ROLLS OF WHITE DRAWING/WRAPPING PAPER,
OLD WHITE RAGS OR AN OLD WHITE T-SHIRT, SCOTCH TAPE, APRON,
OLD SHEET AND FINGER PAINTS.

OBJECTIVES - Using hands to paint is an important sensory experience through which the child learns to feel surfaces, experiment with colors and give free rein to their creativity whilst observing how a stroke of color is generated by each of their gestures. The child will stay focused for a long time as they observe the visually pleasing effects produced by their moves.

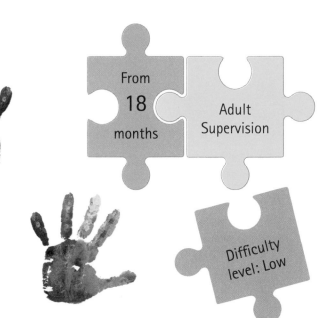

HOW TO DO IT - Choose a sparsely furnished room (better yet a garden or balcony) and clear the floor from rugs and other objects. Dress your child with an overall so that they can get dirty without a problem. If the season allows it, leave the child with minimal clothes underneath. Lay down an old sheet and fasten it with scotch tape to mark the space for the coloring. Place the paint jars along with the sheets of paper, the roll of white wrapping paper, the t-shirt and the pieces of cardboard in the middle of the sheet. Then open the jars and load your finger with a bit of paint and spread it on a piece of cardboard, to help the child understand how the game works. At this point, leave them free to explore colors and surfaces on which they can freely paint using any part of their body.

With younger children, it's nice to take advantage of the colors to learn about the body. So paint their hands, knees and tummy and let the little ones paint us too. It is important to show how they can also paint their feet and leave their footprints on the sheet. It is advisable to begin with a single color, so that they can learn them one at a time, and introduce a new one gradually within the course of a few days.

Recognizing flavors
of fruits and vegetables

MATERIALS

3 BOWLS FILLED WITH 3 DIFFERENT TYPES OF SLICED FRUITS AND VEGETABLES: A SWEET ONE (SUCH AS STRAWBERRY OR BANANA), A SALTY ONE (AN OLIVE, FOR EXAMPLE), AND A SOUR OR BITTER ONE (LEMON, GRAPEFRUIT OR CUCUMBER); BLINDFOLD. FRUITS AND VEGETABLES CAN BE CHOSEN ACCORDING TO PREFERENCE, THE IMPORTANT THING IS TO PRESENT CONTRASTING FLAVORS.

Difficulty level: Low

From **18** months

Adult Supervision

OBJECTIVES - By playing the game of recognizing flavors, the child trains their sense of taste.

HOW TO DO IT - Present the child with a tray containing bowls of fruit and vegetables. Blindfold the child and hand them the first bowl, asking them to tell you its flavor (sweet, salty, bitter or sour), its consistency (hard, soft, creamy), and then what type of fruit or vegetable it is. As the various slices of food can be eaten afterwards, pay careful attention to the shape into which they are cut (avoid the round shape). You can also perform this activity during snack time and prepare a fancy fruit salad with different chunks of fruit.

With young children you can do the same activity but without blindfolding them, or by presenting them with pieces of fruit that they can simply lick, then showing them the entire fruit from which the slice was cut, in order to train their sense of taste and their ability for mental associations.

Recognizing spices by their odor

MATERIALS
6 CLOSED JARS, EACH CONTAINING A FEW TEASPOONS OF SPICE, EITHER POWDERED OR CUT INTO SMALL PIECES. THE SAME SPICES IN THEIR ORIGINAL CONTAINERS. A BLINDFOLD.

OBJECTIVES - Smell is one of the most important but mostly overlooked senses, so it is useful to train the child to distinguish odors and recognize food by smelling. With this activity, the child can also practice awareness, their reflexes and their vocabulary and recognize the objects in the kitchen.

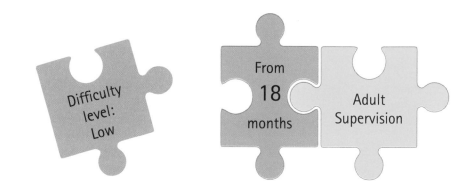

Difficulty level: Low

From **18** months

Adult Supervision

HOW TO DO IT - Show the child the different jars, explaining that each one contains a spice. Also show them the jars with the powdered and whole spices. Blindfold the child and hand them the first jar, asking them to smell its content. Then ask them to describe the odor they smell, their reaction to it, whether or not it is pleasant, whether it is strong or delicate, and then ask them to recognize the spice. At this point, you can pair the jar with the corresponding spice container.

The same activity can be repeated with food of contrasting odors, such as coffee, vinegar, banana, a bag of spiced tea or camomile, honey, olives etc.

Distributing different types of pasta into containers

MATERIALS
4 EMPTY JARS WHERE TO PUT PASTA
OF 4 DIFFERENT SHAPES,
4 CONTAINERS (EACH HOLDING
A DOZEN PIECES OF PASTA),
1 SALAD BOWL.

OBJECTIVES - This is an activity
involving selection and classification,
which stimulates the child's
categorical thinking and exercises
their visual recognition, their
selective attention and fine motor
skills.

HOW TO DO IT - Drop a piece of pasta into each empty jar in order to mark the type of pasta that each one must contain. Ask the child to redistribute the pieces of pasta into their corresponding jars. Afterwards, you can repeat the activity by mixing all types of pasta into a single bowl – a salad

bowl, for example – and then ask the child once again to redistribute them in the various jars, in which you have already inserted the piece of pasta that serves as a model (which helps the child check for error and correct themselves).

Making stamps out of potatoes

MATERIALS

3 SOFT POTATOES (A BIT OLD, THE ONES YOU WOULD NO LONGER EAT), A KNIFE OR A PAPER CUTTER, SHEETS OF PAPER, TEMPERA PAINTS, PAPER PLATES FOR THE PAINTS, STENCILS (COOKIE CUTTERS ARE EQUALLY GOOD) OR CARDBOARD.

OBJECTIVES - This activity helps the child understand the concept of front and back, develops fine motor skills and hand-to-eye coordination, and enhances creativity.

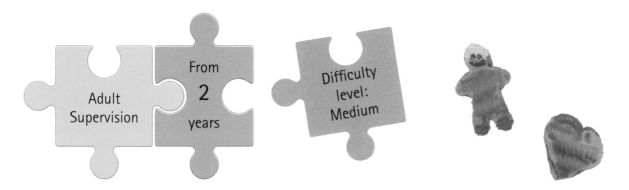

HOW TO DO IT - Cut the potato in half; depending on their age, the child can do it by themselves, or you can simply make them help you by asking them to pass you the objects and observe what you are doing. Then take a cookie cutter and press it into the potato's flesh until it creates a shape. Remove the flesh around the cutter so that it appears in relief. The stamp is ready. Do the same with the other potatoes, letting the child try on their own, depending on age. Do not be afraid to let them use the knife with your supervision. Show them how to use it, how to hold it without cutting themselves and how to press down on the potato to cut it in half. Then pour the tempera paint into the saucer and place it on the child's right (always work from left to right), next to a piece of paper. Take your potato, dip it in the color, and press it on the sheet. There's your stamp!

With this method, you can also compose words by drawing a letter on the stamp instead. If you do not have the proper cutters, you can easily make them: draw the shapes of letters or numbers in pencil on the cardboard, then cut them out. Now lay the cardboard shape at the center of the potato's flesh and cut the potato with the cutter, removing the flesh around the

figure to shape it in relief. You can make any kind of shape!

In case of younger children, you can make them touch the relief on the potato's surface with their finger, make an imprint on their hand, and have them try to stamp the sheet, thus exercising movements with their hands and wrists.

Decanting liquids and solids

MATERIALS

VARIOUS TYPES OF CONTAINERS OF DIFFERENT SHAPES AND MATERIALS, VARIOUS TYPES OF
DECANTERS OF DIFFERENT SHAPES AND MATERIALS, MATERIALS TO TRANSFER (RICE, LEGUMES, FLOUR,
PASTA, SAND, PEBBLES, PINE CONES, HAZELNUTS, ACORNS, CHESTNUTS, CAPS AND LIQUIDS).

OBJECTIVES - This is a very important activity for eye-to-hand coordination as it helps the child develop good muscular control, calibrate their movements, hold thin objects properly in their hands and train their hands for writing.

HOW TO DO IT - Decanting is an activity that can be done with any type of object of various size and consistency, whether solid or liquid, and by using various instruments. When using different kitchen utensils and tools to transfer materials, children have an opportunity to grasp how these work and learn how to use them to move material without spilling it. It is good to begin with simple grabbing tools and then move on to more sophisticated ones, such as tongs. It's also advisable to initially stick with objects of medium size. Once coordination improves, smaller objects can be proposed. There's an advantage to suggesting that the transfer always be made from left to right, as it follows the direction of writing. Arrange the materials in front of the child and show them how to transfer objects or liquids from one container into another. Make them observe what to do in case some material spills during the decanting, and how to clean the spilled material.

There are plenty of opportunities for transfers during food preparation: make the child transfer pieces of fried meat, pieces of fruit salad, pasta that needs to be boiled and soup greens into pots or dishes; make them use tongs to drop meat or vegetables into a pan, scoop out ice cream, pour grated cheese, etc.

This is also a great activity for younger children, who can do it with bare hands, then experiment with controlling a spoon, then a teaspoon, and finally the tongs.

Creating a rainbow out
of fruit

MATERIALS
6 LITTLE BOWLS, 2 WOODEN SKEWERS, 2 STRAWBERRIES, 2 ORANGE SEGMENTS, 2 BANANA SLICES, 2 PIECES OF KIWI FRUIT, 2 BLUEBERRIES, 2 PURPLE GRAPES, A DRAWING OF A RAINBOW. FRUIT CAN VARY ACCORDING TO PREFERENCE; THE IMPORTANT THING IS THAT THE COLORS BE RED, ORANGE, YELLOW, GREEN, BLUE AND VIOLET.

OBJECTIVES - The best way to learn colors is by experimenting with associations between colors and real objects, such as fruit. In this activity the child easily learns the colors of the rainbow, while exercising fine motor skills.

HOW TO DO IT - You can seize a snack opportunity in suggesting to the child how to create a fruit kebab with the colors of the rainbow. Place a tray with the bowls containing the fruit pieces and skewer before the child. Place a photo or a drawing of a rainbow next to the tray and begin describing the colors of the rainbow from top to bottom. Then repeat the first color, look for the piece of fruit in the corresponding color ("red like a strawberry"), and stick it on the skewer, showing the child how to insert the tip of the skewer into the pulp of the fruit. Then hand the skewer to the child and let them continue.

In the case of younger children, it may be practical for you to hold the skewer and have the child insert the piece of fruit.

Recognizing sounds

MATERIALS

6 CANS, A BLINDFOLD, A HANDFUL OF SEEDS, BEANS, CHICKPEAS, PEBBLES, CORN, RICE, PASTA AND ANY MATERIAL YOU FIND THAT CAN PRODUCE DIFFERENT AND INTERESTING SOUNDS WHEN SHAKEN INSIDE A CONTAINER.

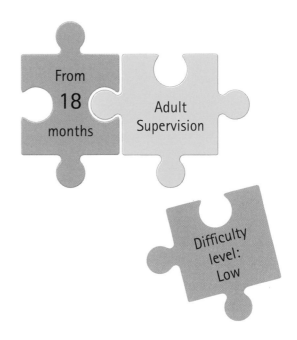

OBJECTIVES

- Here is another activity to stimulate the child's senses - this time that of hearing - while practicing auditive discrimination, selective attention, auditive memory and vocabulary.

HOW TO DO IT

- This is a fun activity to do with your child. Show the child the objects you have chosen and distribute them in 6 containers. Then, taking the containers one by one, tell the child the word for the material it contains (for example, "beans"), and shake the container 3 times in order to let the child listen to the sound made by the object ("listen to this noise: it's the beans"). Once you have listened to all the sounds, blindfold the child and tell them to pay close attention to the sound that they hear and to tell you what material it is.

With older children you can likewise seize this occasion to enhance vocabulary by describing sounds together (sharp, low, loud, soft, long or short), then urging them to use these terms to describe the sound that they hear during the game.

Younger children, on the other hand, can simply use containers by shaking them and creating their own music. Supervise them, so that they do not stick small pieces into their mouth or nose.

You can repeat the activity with other objects or even with musical items, such as bells with different sounds.

Learning with an activity panel

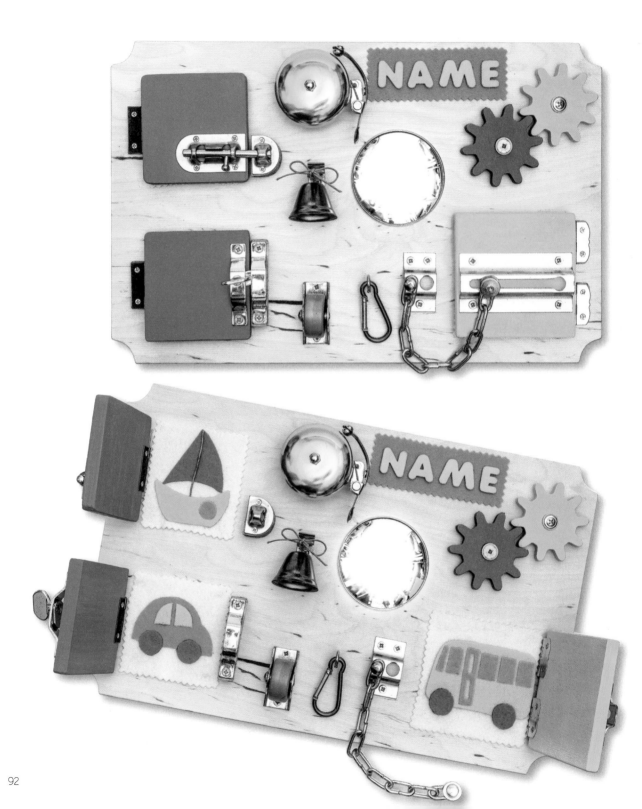

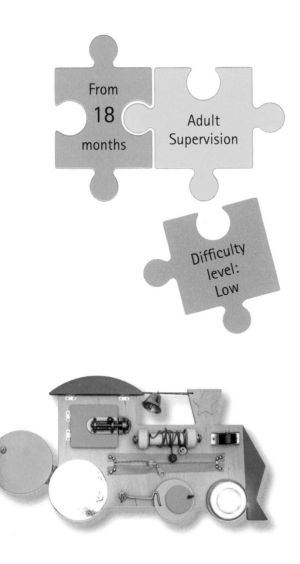

From **18** months

Adult Supervision

Difficulty level: Low

MATERIALS

A WOODEN PANEL, WOOD GLUE, HINGES, DOOR HINGES, STRINGS, BOLTS, PADLOCKS, ON/OFF SWITCHES, BUTTONS, BELL PUSHES, KNOCKERS, LITTLE BELLS, WHEELS, A FAUCET, BUTTONHOLES AND BUTTONS, PIECES OF FABRIC AND ANY SORTS OF REDUCED-SCALE ITEMS FOUND IN THE HOUSE, IN HARDWARE STORE, ODDS-AND-ENDS OR DRY-GOODS STORES.

OBJECTIVES -Exercise fine motor skills in a specific manner, exercise precision of movements, stimulate concentration and problem solving.

HOW TO DO IT - You can buy a ready-made panel in toy stores or easily make it yourself. All you need to do is glue all the reduced-scale items that call for manual action (opening / closing, unscrewing, hooking, inserting, rotating, threading, etc. ...) on a wooden panel. You can also vary the objects according to the child's development stage and interests.

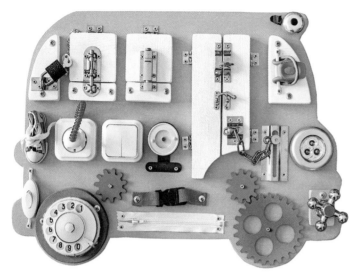

Place the panel on a table in front of the child and leave them free to try out the different activities by themselves. The child will be guided by their curiosity and interests. They may therefore be attracted to the strings, or the padlocks or the hinges; they will want to open and shut little windows or slip on a tiny bolt. Let them learn how to use the different materials by themselves and intervene only if they request it, acting as a model. Let them repeat their actions innumerable times, and do not correct them if they make a mistake: thanks to various active attempts, the child will be able to consolidate what they have learned. Some activities may be more difficult than others, depending on the child's phase of development. Do not rush them; the child will work their way through the panel in due course.

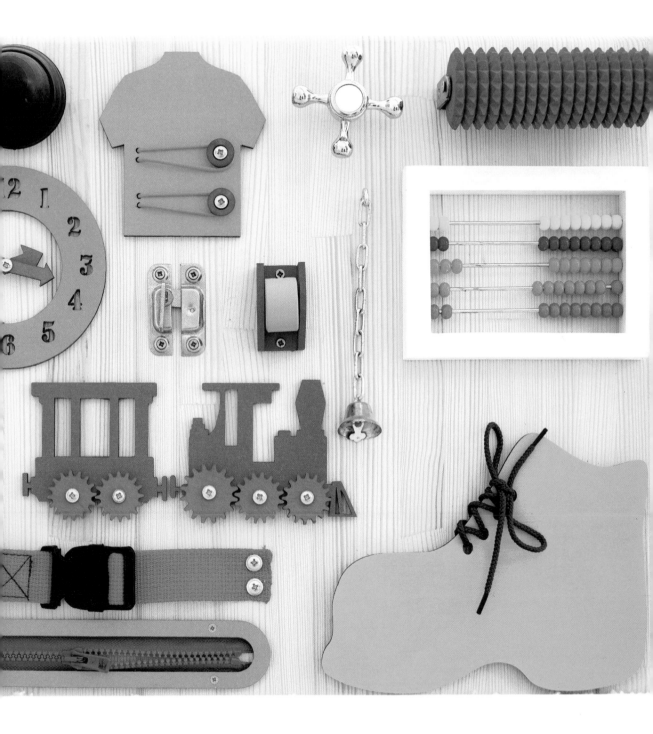

PRACTICAL LIFE
EXPERIENCES

Washing hands by oneself

MATERIALS

BAR OF SOAP OR LIQUID SOAP, BASIN,
WATER JUG, TOWEL.

OBJECTIVES - The act of washing hands is one of the most important daily personal hygiene activities to teach the child.

HOW TO DO IT - First, it is useful to show the child how to wash their hands. Place a bar of soap (or a liquid-soap dispenser), a basin, a jug of warm water and a hand towel from left to right in

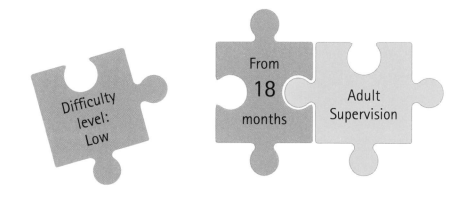

front of the child. Pour warm water into the basin, wet your hands, take the soap and begin to rub it between your hands. Then, put it back in its place and continue sliding your hands against each other. Describe each step verbally, making each movement slowly so that the child is able to see them all well. After about a minute, stick your hands in the basin and rinse off the soap. Once they look clean, make a few movements to shake off drops of water, then take the towel and dry them. Now ask the child to repeat the sequence of your gestures.

Once the child has understood how to wash their hands, you can proceed to let them do so at the sink (reachable with a stool), substituting the basin with the sink, so that the child already has water to wash their hands in after they have soaped them. It's useful to make the child observe how the water's color changes after the hands have

been washed, as this give them a sense of the dirt's transitory quality. Hang a towel within the child's reach, so they can dry their hands by themselves. We can also ask the child to smell their hands after washing them so that they may appreciate the smell of soap on clean hands. Establish fixed moments in the day when the child must always wash their hands, so that this becomes a routine and the child themselves remembers to go and wash them.

Brushing teeth by oneself

MATERIALS
TOOTHBRUSH, TOOTHPASTE, A CUP, A MIRROR, A BOTTLE OF WATER, AND A TOWEL.

OBJECTIVES - Brushing teeth is an important personal hygiene activity too, which the child must learn to do three times a day.

HOW TO DO IT - In this case, too, begin by providing an example of the procedure that must be followed, then brush your teeth in front of the child in slow motion. Then, ask them to do it with you. Set the materials before the child and begin. Fill the cup with water and place it on the child's right, then take the toothbrush and ask the child to hold it in whichever hand feels more comfortable, and,

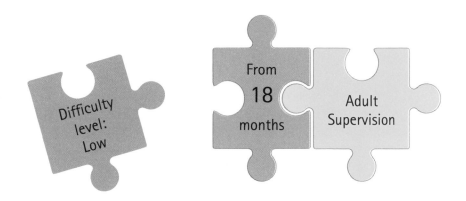

Difficulty level: Low

From **18** months

Adult Supervision

with the other hand to squeeze out a bit of toothpaste, with your help if necessary. Prepare your toothbrush and brush your teeth together. Turn towards the mirror and brush your teeth looking at yourself in the mirror; the child will do the same. You can use a small hourglass to measure the length of time needed to brush teeth. Once you are finished, rinse the toothbrush in the cup and put it back in its place, then rinse the remaining toothpaste from your mouth and dry it with the towel. Explain to the child how important it is to brush their teeth to keep them clean and healthy. Remember to set up a fixed routine to brush them, so that the child may remember to do so by themselves.

Getting dressed by oneself

MATERIALS
JACKET, SHIRT WITH BUTTONS AND BUTTONHOLES, JERSEY WITH SNAPS, PANTS, ZIPPED SWEATSHIRT, T-SHIRT.

OBJECTIVES
One of the greatest sources of satisfaction for the child is to be able to get dressed by themselves – a complex activity that requires eye-to-hand coordination, the planning of sequential movements, agility and knowledge of the body's structure.

HOW TO DO IT
Putting on various pieces of clothing requires different actions. Start by letting the child experiment with the possibility of undressing on their own, and of helping them get dressed. Also make them practice with zippers and buttons. Lay the unbuttoned shirt down on a table and allow the child to fasten and unfasten the buttons in the buttonholes or with snaps. Show them how to do so with slow movements while verbally explaining each action. Do the same with the zipper. Then make them dress themselves and practice with different clothes. **Jersey:** to put on a jersey, lay it on a table, with its front facing down and its bottom facing the child. Push the child into the shirt with their arms raised until they reach the neckline. Then have them insert their arms into the sleeves and finally push their head out.

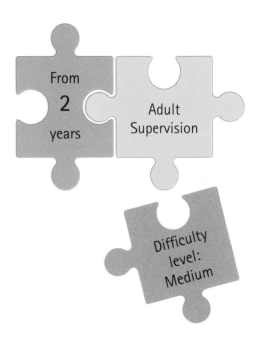

From
2
years

Adult Supervision

Difficulty level: Medium

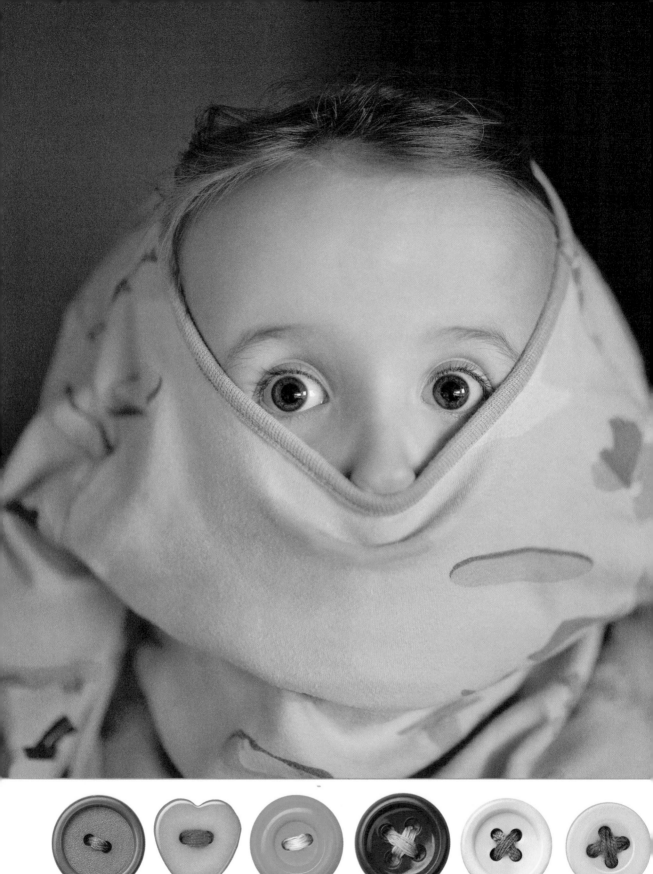

This will take a bit of practice, but it will bring great satisfaction to the child!

Pants: lay the pants on the floor with their legs wide open, then let the child slide their bare feet into the two spaces. At this point, you merely have to bend down, grab the edge of the pants, pull them up, and you're done. Begin with soft pants, which are easier to put on.

Jacket: put on the jacket with the inside facing up and its top at the child's side. Make the child bend forward, keeping their head down to put their arms into the jacket. Then lifting the jacket with the arms, push the child's arms slightly behind their head, so that the jacket can pass over the neck and onto the back. Describe the procedure step by step, and show the child how to perform the action several times.

Matching socks

MATERIALS

SIX PAIRS OF DIFFERENT COLORED SOCKS.

OBJECTIVES - This is an activity that develops visual recognition and exercises fine motor skills.

HOW TO DO IT - Place the socks inside a container in random order. Take any sock and describe its color (e.g. "it's blue"). Pick up another one and do the same thing, then put it next to the last one, thus creating a row of socks. Explain that it's necessary to look for socks of the same color. Every time a socks is the same color as one of the others, do not place it on the side but over the matching sock. Eventually you'll be left with 6 pairs of socks.

Difficulty
level:
Low

From
2
years

Adult
Supervision

Let the child have fun looking for matching socks, and suggest the activity with variously patterned socks as well. Very young children will simply arrange the socks in a row, but by observing you pairing them, they will begin imitating you once they feel ready.

From the age of 3, the child can also learn how to fold matching socks. To practice this, take an old pair of socks and draw three lines at the points where the sock should be folded, explaining to the child that they must fold the sock precisely along these lines. Let them try to do so over and over again.

Putting socks on

MATERIALS
2 PAIRS OF ANKLE SOCKS, ONE FOR US, ONE FOR THE CHILD.

OBJECTIVES - Putting on socks is a rather complex action, which requires much eye-to-hand coordination and the ability to apply motor skills to a series of actions.

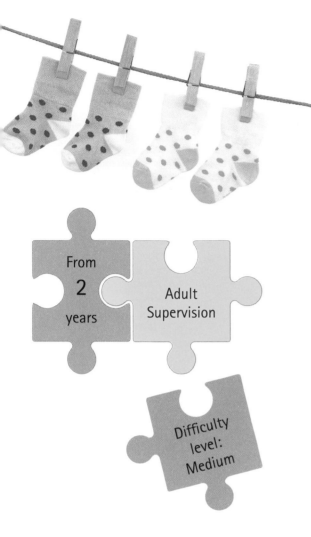

From **2** years

Adult Supervision

Difficulty level: Medium

HOW TO DO IT - Show the child how a sock is constructed, indicating the part for the toes and the part for the heel. Sit down on the floor and put a sock in front of you, with the opening towards you. Pick up the sock with your hands and stick your toes inside to stretch the opening. Keeping it open, insert your foot and let it advance to the end. Pull up the sock and you're done. Explain each action out loud as you perform it, making slow and precise gestures. Then make the child try; by trying and retrying, they will find their own way of putting socks on.

Lacing shoes

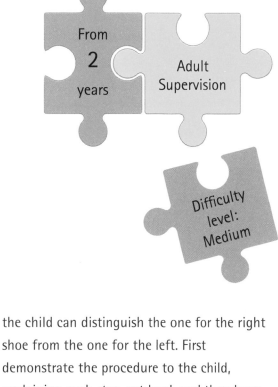

From **2** years

Adult Supervision

Difficulty level: Medium

MATERIALS
A WOODEN FRAME (OR A SHOE BOX), A PIECE OF FABRIC, SCISSORS, TWO SHOELACES OF DIFFERENT COLORS.

OBJECTIVES - Lacing shoes requires careful eye-to-hand coordination, fine muscular control, concentration and the ability to plan a sequence of actions. This is a highly complex activity, which can be performed from around the age of 3, though it can be practiced earlier.

HOW TO DO IT - It is useful to get the child to practice lacing shoes on a lacing frame. This can also be made at home: these are wooden frames, across which we can stretch a cloth with holes pierced along two parallel rows. The child must thread the laces through the holes. In this way they can learn and easily practice the procedure for threading laces, making a knot, and finally, making a bow. It's also possible to take a shoe box, turn it upside down, drill two rows of holes in it, and thread the laces through these holes. You can do the same with an egg carton or a roll of toilet paper.
Choose two shoelaces of different color, so

the child can distinguish the one for the right shoe from the one for the left. First demonstrate the procedure to the child, explaining each step out loud, and then have the child repeat it. Once the child has been trained, you can make them practice with their shoes on.
Younger children will have fun simply trying to thread and pull laces through the holes.

Spreading jam

MATERIALS
SLICE OF BREAD, SMALL KNIFE WITH A ROUND TIP, TEASPOON, JAR OF JAM.

OBJECTIVES - Spreading jam is an activity that develops eye-to-hand coordination, fine motor skills, and concentration.It requires calibrating the amount of pressure exerted by the knife on the bread, carrying jam without letting it fall, an ability to balance and good coordination.

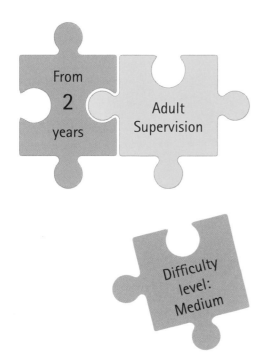

From **2** years

Adult Supervision

Difficulty level: Medium

HOW TO DO IT - Place a jar of jam, a teaspoon, a slice of bread and a napkin for cleaning leftover food in a row in front of the child. Show the child how to fill the spoon with jam and gently spread it on the bread. Have them repeat the action. Then take the round knife and show the child how to hold the bread in their non-dominant hand and gently spread the jam on the bread from left to right with their other hand. After performing this activity, the child can eat the sandwich, so choose a jam that they like.

You can then repeat the same sequence of actions with dry toast and a cookie, which are more difficult types of food as their surface is thinner and easily breakable. You will therefore have to teach the child to pay attention to the amount of force exerted by the knife on the toast or biscuit while the jam is being spread so that they can learn to calibrate the intensity of their strength.

Loading a washing machine and hanging clothes

MATERIALS
BASKET OF DIRTY CLOTHES, WASHING MACHINE, DETERGENT, PLASTIC CUP OR JAR, TEASPOON.

OBJECTIVES - Make the child participate in everyday life activities, help cultivate their sense of security and confidence in their ability and train their attitude for logic. Through the activity of doing the laundry, the child learns what it means to pass from the condition of dirtiness to cleanliness, exercises manual dexterity by measuring the detergent and learns how to follow a sequence of actions that lead to a result.

HOW TO DO IT - First of all, it is important for the child to learn that there's a basket in the house for them to put their dirty clothes in. There's one for the child and one for the parents.

Then teach the child that the dirt is removed with soap, like when we wash our own hands. You can then try proving to the child the meaning of the transition from dirtiness to cleanliness by taking a handkerchief, drawing a small spot on it with a marker, then showing how the stain disappears when it is rubbed with laundry soap (e.g. Marseilles soap). Have the child rub the soap on the stain; this will be a fun activity and useful for developing their fine motor skills and training their wrist. Finally rinse the soap off the handkerchief in a basin of water. Then make the child notice how clean the handkerchief is and that the stain is gone, while the water is cloudy.

Once you have demonstrated the concept of cleaning, you can introduce the meaning of the washing machine. You can present it as a machine that soaps the clothes and rinses them by itself, thus removing stains.

Take the basket of dirty clothes and your child in front of the washing machine. Put one garment at a time in the washing machine; start doing so yourself, then let the child continue.

Take the cup and ask the child to pour in a teaspoon of detergent, or as much as you feel necessary based on the amount of clothing that needs to be washed.

Now ask the child to slowly and gently pour the detergent in the cup into the appropriate container of the washing machine. Explain to the child that the soap is inserted there in the form of powder and will dissolve in the water and into the clothes while the washing machine is in operation.

With a child over 2 years of age, show the sequence of buttons that need to be pressed while explaining the function of each one.

Specify to the child that they need to decide how hot the wash water should be in order to clean the clothes. Then make the child memorize the sequence of actions, reminding them what they did when washing the handkerchief: they had poured in the soap, rubbed the stain and rinsed it off, so they have to insert the soap in the washing machine too, program the temperature of the water and determine how long the washing machine should soap and rinse

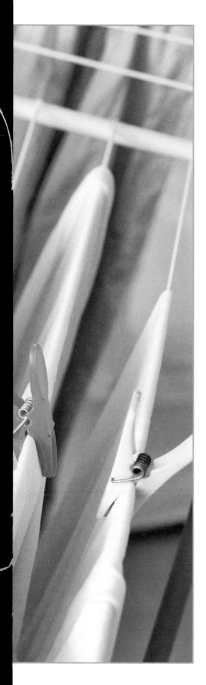

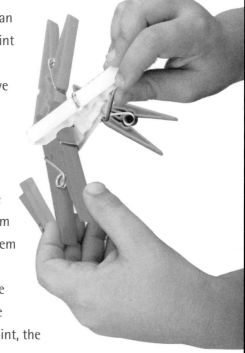

the clothes for. At this point you can turn on your washing machine. Point out to the child the noise it makes while washing and let them observe the churning clothes through the door so that they become even more aware of how the washing process unfolds.

When the wash is done, ask the child to pull out all the clothes from the washing machine and place them in a basin. Let the child look and smell them so that they may notice their cleanliness and thus reinforce the concept of cleaning. At this point, the clothes are ready to be hung.

With a very young child, you can simply make them help you put the clothes in the washing machine and pour in the detergent.

In order to hang clothes, the child must learn how to open and close clothes pegs. Let them practice this activity by giving them a basket of pegs and asking them to clip them onto the basket's rim. Show them how to squeeze the clip between their fingers and open it by pressing lightly.

Once the child has become familiar with this operation, allow them to hang some simple garments. You can extend a rope or nylon string between two chairs, so that it will be at the child's height. Hand the child handkerchiefs, napkins, bibs, underwear and socks and let them hang them. Show them once how to do it: pick up a sock and press it against the string with one hand; use the other hand - the dominant one - to pick up a peg, open it and snap it shut on the sock, attaching it to the string. Always explain each action that you perform. Now let the child try and try again, until they can coordinate their actions and do the precise movement.

Sharpening pencils

MATERIALS
TWO PENCIL SHARPENERS,
TWO UNSHARPENED PENCILS,
TWO SHEETS OF PAPER.

OBJECTIVES - Sharpening a pencil is a very simple and quick task that requires little time but a great deal of fine motor skill and eye-to-hand coordination.

HOW TO DO IT - Place the pencil sharpeners to the left of the child and the pencils on top of the sheets of paper to their right. Explain to the child what you are about to do, specifying that the sharpener is an object that must be used carefully because it has a blade and is used for cutting.

First, demonstrate how to sharpen the pencil, making slow movements and explaining them out loud. Then let the child try to sharpen the pencil while you are doing the same, so that they can observe your movements well and imitate them. Keep the sharpener firmly in one hand and with the dominant hand stick the pencil into the hole. Explain that one must press lightly and turn the pencil in the opposite direction of the sharpener's blade so that the pencil point can be sharpened. As soon as the child sees the first shavings coming out of the sharpener, they will quickly understand that their actions are correct and will repeat them. If, however, the pencil just spins around and around, then they will understand that they are doing something wrong.

Finally, pull the pencil out of the sharpener and shake it to see the shavings fall on the paper; this way the child will become aware of the change in the condition of the pencil, which now has a point. You can repeat the action with variously colored pencils.

Washing salad

MATERIALS
LETTUCE, COLANDER, BAG,
SALAD SPINNER, SALAD BOWL.

From **18** months

Adult Supervision

Difficulty level: Low

OBJECTIVES - Here is another activity that engages the child in everyday life, allows for the development of fine motor skills and the ability to plan sequential actions.

HOW TO DO IT - This is a simple activity, which the child can easily carry out even by themselves once we have shown them what to do. Take a head of lettuce and lay it on a plate, placing a bag and a colander to the child's right. Place a salad spinner and a salad bowl further to the side. Show the child how to tear away the outer leaves of the lettuce while holding the lettuce in one hand and the leaf in the other. Put the outermost leaves that are unsuitable for eating inside the bag. Put the others in the colander. Have the child repeat this action. Once all the leaves have been detached, wash them under running water, showing the child how to wash them carefully and eliminate the residues of dirt.

Have the child repeat the operation. Finally, place the leaves in the salad spinner and let them observe how it is used. The child will have fun trying to rotate the salad spinner quickly by themselves. Make the child notice how much water has been removed through the rotation of the knob. Place the salad into the salad bowl.

Shelling peas and trimming beans

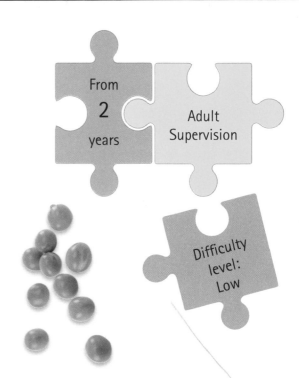

From **2** years

Adult Supervision

Difficulty level: Low

MATERIALS
A PLATE OF PEAS INSIDE THEIR PODS, A PLATE OF RAW GREEN BEANS, A CUP, A COLANDER, POSSIBLY A PAIR OF SCISSORS.

OBJECTIVES - This is a very useful activity because it works on fine motor skills and eye-to-hand coordination.

HOW TO DO IT - **In the case of the peas,** place a plate with peas on a tray before the child and a cup next to it. Take a pod and show the child how to open it by pulling at its filaments, and afterwards how to shell the peas, making them fall one after another into the cup. Leave the pods in the dish and discard them at the end of the process, or keep them for another recipe.

In the case of the green beans, place a plate with green beans on a tray before the child, then a cup and a colander. Pick up a bean and show the child how to break its ends; then place these in the cup and drop the green bean into the colander. Ask the child to repeat the operation. Accept the fact that they may be inaccurate and may not properly clean all the beans; the important thing is that they practice nipping then grasping the string bean between their thumb and forefinger and exerting force to break off the part of the green bean that will be

discarded. You can also repeat the activity by using a small pair of scissors to snip the ends in order to train the child how to use scissors. Once the job is done, rinse the beans under the water and put them in a pot. They will be happy to eat the green beans they have been prepared with their own hands!

Cutting fruit

MATERIALS
BANANA, A KNIFE WITH A ROUNDED BLADE, PEAR,
APPLE, LEMON, A POINTED KNIFE.

OBJECTIVES - The activity of cutting fruit exercises fine manual skills, control over movements of the hand and the wrist and eye-to-hand coordination.

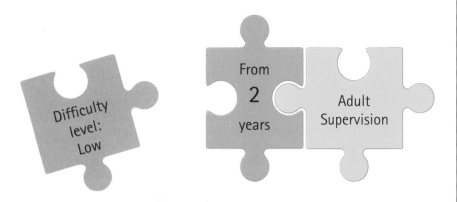

Difficulty level: Low

From 2 years

Adult Supervision

HOW TO DO IT - Begin with a rounded-blade knife, such as the one used to cut cheese or spread butter, which is safe for the child. Before beginning the activity, explain to the child how a knife is made so that they learn how to handle the object with care, because it could be dangerous. Place a soft fruit - a banana would be ideal - on a tray in front of the child. Place the knife next to them. Show the child how to hold the knife and dig it into the pulp of the banana in order to produce a slice. Make them repeat the action along the entire length of the banana.

With older children, you can then re-propose the activity with other types of fruits with various textures: pears, lemons, apples. In this case you should use a sharp knife. Always make the child watch how it is done first, then have them repeat the operation; with a little practice, they will develop good coordination in the movements of their wrist. Once the child becomes familiar with the activity, you can suggest working with other kitchen utensils, such as an apple corer. You can prepare a fruit salad together, which the child will eat with great satisfaction, having prepared it themselves.

Peeling onions and garlic

MATERIALS
A BOWL WITH AN ONION INSIDE, A BOWL WITH A HEAD OF GARLIC INSIDE, AN EMPTY BOWL,
A SMALL KNIFE, AND A CHOPPING BOARD.

OBJECTIVES - The skin of onions and garlic is so thin that it must be peeled with great care; this is therefore an excellent exercise for developing fine motor skills and eye-to-hand coordination.

HOW TO DO IT - Set the materials before the child, placing the bowls on their left and the chopping board - which will be the child's work surface - on their right. Show the child how to take the onion and cut a wedge out of it; then show them how to gently remove its dry skin, which will

break away, so all the residue has to be carefully removed. Then take the head of garlic and show the child how to slice the top and separate the cloves.

Then make them remove the skin from the cloves.

Older children can even slice the onion and the garlic cloves that they have peeled. Remind the child to wash their hands after touching this food.

Break and beat eggs

MATERIALS

A BOWL WITH 3 EGGS INSIDE, AN EMPTY BOWL, A HIGH-RIMMED BOWL,
A SPONGE FOR CLEANING UP EGG DRIPS, A WHISK OR A FORK.

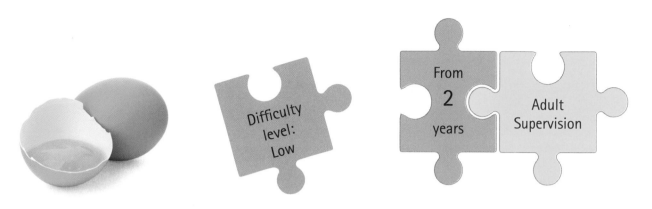

OBJECTIVES - This activity is fairly complex and is therefore a good exercise for mobilizing the wrist and the hand, developing hand-to eye coordination, controlling force and increasing the accuracy of motor gestures. These household tasks are important training for writing and using a pen.

HOW TO DO IT - Present the child with the materials arranged on a tray in an orderly manner – lined up from left to right in order of use. It is necessary to explain to the child the delicacy of an egg, which is a fragile food that must be handled with care and can very easily break. This means that the child must learn to calibrate the force of their hand movements and gestures. Take one egg and gently tap it against the rim of the large bowl and allow the child to watch it crack. Let the child observe how cracks are made in the egg shell. As soon as the egg white begins to empty out, open the shell and pour the contents into the bowl. Then throw the shell into the empty bowl. Ask the child to repeat your actions with the remaining eggs. Once all the eggs are in the

bowl, you can beat them with a whisk. Show the child how to tilt the bowl and make circular movements, always in the same direction, by rotating the whisk (or fork) with the wrist. In fact, this is an activity that develops the rotatory ability of the wrist very well.

Accept that the child will make mistakes and get into trouble, and therefore let them try over and over again.

Baking cookies

MATERIALS

8.8 OZ FLOUR, 4.4 OZ BUTTER, 3.5 OZ CANE SUGAR, 1 EGG AND A PINCH OF SALT,
COOKIE CUTTERS, A BEAKER, ROLLING PIN, BAKING TRAY WITH PARCHMENT PAPER,
A TEA TOWEL, A KITCHEN APRON.

OBJECTIVES - This is a complex activity that exercises both various fine motor skills and the ability to plan actions to reach a goal.

HOW TO DO IT - As there are endless recipes for baking cookies, let's choose a very simple and quick one. Use a wide table, before which the child can stand by your side. Place the already weighed ingredients on the table and arrange them in the order of use. Take the flour and pour it on the table, making the child help you. Then, have the child pick up the ingredients one by one and add them to the dough. Finally, let them break the egg and pour all of it in. Begin kneading with energetic movements to show how it should be done. Then let the child have fun kneading the short pastry with their little hands. At the end, shape it into a ball and let it rest under the tea towel for about an hour. In the meantime, make the child wash their hands and help you figure out the work plan. When the hour is up, roll out the pastry with a rolling pin. This, too, is an action that the child can do. Take some cookie cutters, or a glass that can be used as a cutter, and let the child cut out several shapes in the pastry. Arrange all the cookies on the baking tray and put them in the oven for about 15-20 minutes a 356 °F (180 °C). Once they are baked, let them cool and decorate them however you like.

This is an activity that can be done even with very young children, from 18 months on, by tailoring the proposed activity to the child's level; so, for example, they may be able to sprinkle the flour on the board, pass the bowls with the ingredients or press a cookie cutter into the dough.

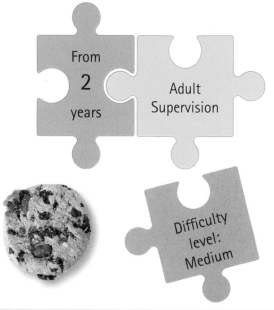

From
2
years

Adult
Supervision

Difficulty
level:
Medium

Setting the table

MATERIALS
PLATES, CUPS, SILVERWARE, A WHITE A3-SIZE SHEET OF PAPER, A FELT-TIP PEN.

Difficulty level: Low

From 2 years

Adult Supervision

OBJECTIVES - This activity teaches the how to perform a complex action, develops an understanding of left/right, increases their vocabulary and practices memorizing and hand-to-eye coordination.

HOW TO DO IT - In order to set up the table, it's important that the child has already learnt the words for the single objects, at least the word for plate, glass, knife and fork. To begin with, take a fairly large A3-sized sheet of paper and trace the shape of a plate in the middle, of a fork on the left, of a knife on the right and of a glass at the top. Place the drawn sheet on the table before the cutlery and the plate. Pick up the plate and let the child notice its shape and run their finger along its perimeter and then run it along the one in the drawing, to show that they are identical. Then lay the plate on the drawing and let the child proceed with the tableware. The child will have to compare the shape of the real object with that of the drawn object. In addition, ask them to say the name of the tableware they are placing on the sheet out loud in order to reinforce their understanding of the vocabulary. You can then add other objects to the drawing, such as a teaspoon for fruit, a glass or two

forks. You can then proceed to ask the child to set the table with the sheet next to them, so that they no longer have to place the objects on the sheet, but simply use it as a model.

With younger children, you can work on having them recognize the tableware first, and then let them watch you as you place them over the shapes on the sheet.

OUTDOOR ACTIVITIES

Discovering nature

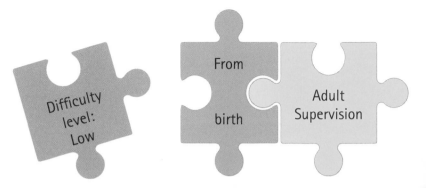

MATERIALS

MATERIALS FOR DIGGING,
A MAGNIFYING GLASS,
NOTEBOOK AND PENCIL, CAMERA.

OBJECTIVES - Experiencing and living in touch with nature is a 360-degree sensory experience that offers opportunities for simultaneous auditory, tactile, visual and taste stimulation, along with other opportunities to practice both fine and ordinary movements; the child learns to appreciate order, silence, patience, respect for other living creatures, the passing of time and change.

HOW TO DO IT - Different things can be experienced in nature, so here are some suggestions. Take the time to go out for a walk in a park, stroll down a road, explore a garden or go visit a vegetable garden or farm.

Without rushing, devote time to exploring the environment, allowing the child to directly experience the smells of flowers, wet grass, mud, plants; to remain silent and listen to the sounds of insects, falling rain, wind rustling

through the leaves; to experience the texture of leaves, trunks and soil, as well as to taste berries, a freshly picked apple, fresh milk, etc. Depending on the season, you can go to a park or a nearby forest to gather acorns, sticks, stones and pine cones. You can look for elements in nature based on pre-selected criteria (for example, all objects of a specific color or shape); you can observe how a flower is constructed, collect leaves of different shapes, collect stones of various color and size.

You can also take advantage of outdoor spaces to engage in movement: climbing rocks, balancing on a stone path, hanging from branches, jumping in puddles, engaging in chasing games, or rolling on grass or sand.

Do not be afraid to take children outdoors even on overcast days; let them experience all sorts of weather conditions. The important thing is that they are dressed in suitable clothes.

If you want, you can give the child a magnifying glass with which they can explore and observe the veins of leaves, the labor of ants or the elements that compose soil from up close. Or you can give them a camera to capture what attracts them or a notebook where to draw actual objects that are of interest to them.

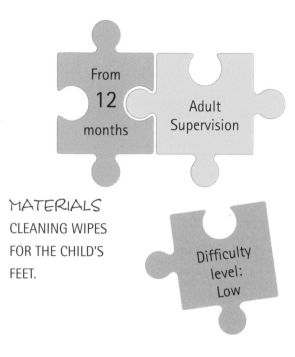

From **12** months

Adult Supervision

MATERIALS
CLEANING WIPES
FOR THE CHILD'S
FEET.

Difficulty level: Low

OBJECTIVES - Stimulate the child's sensory development.

HOW TO DO IT - Allow the child to experience new sensations and be in contact with nature.

Choose a setting where you feel comfortable, such as a garden lawn, a beach or a gravel path. Remove the shoes from your child, leaving them free to walk around. Stroke their feet with a blade of grass, then with a rock and ask them what sensations they feel. Let them get dirty, walk on tiptoe on uncomfortable ground and relax the soles of their feet on soft grass. Prepare a small sensorial journey, in which the child can walk on various surfaces - hard, rough, cold, soft and warm. Then ask the child to describe how their feet feel so they can learn to pay attention to their sensations.

Walking barefoot

First contact with outdoor animals

OBJECTIVES - It is important that children learn to appreciate animals from an early age, because by approaching an animal, the child learns to be respectful, to move slowly, to keep their voice down and to respect the distance that the animal wishes to keep. In addition, it's an opportunity for expanding vocabulary, learning the words for animals and their body parts.

HOW TO DO IT - Opportunities for coming into contact with animals may be random, or you can create them intentionally. It can be useful to simply stop and observe the animals that live around us every time an opportunity arises: a sparrow on a tree, a pigeon on a bench, a cat on a curb, a dog with its owner, a fish in a pond and so on. Let the child observe the animal; teach them to keep their voice

MATERIALS
ILLUSTRATED BOOKS ABOUT
ANIMALS OR PHOTOGRAPHS
OF ANIMALS, CAMERA.

Difficulty level: Low

From 12 months

Adult Supervision

down and move slowly so as not to alarm the animal. Teach them that if the animal does not wish to be approached, its will must be respected. You can feed the pigeons in the square or the fish in the pond. You can visit a farm and observe live animals that you and the child have previously observed in a book. You can organize a trip to the mountains and search for local animals like goats.

In the case of older children, you can take photos of animals and later look for information about them at home – how they are born, what they eat and interesting facts on their way of life. If you lucky enough to be living with a pet, then actively involve the child in the animal's care. Learning from an early age to take care of another living being is an experience that teaches respect and stimulates empathy.

Looking for ants

MATERIALS
A MAGNIFYING GLASS.

OBJECTIVES - This is an activity that mainly stimulates the power of observation, selective attention, concentration, and teaches anticipation, patience, silence and respect for other living beings.

HOW TO DO IT - An example of an animal that can easily be observed outdoors is the ant. You can choose a corner in a courtyard or a garden where to look for these tiny creatures. You can go outside and assign the child the task of finding and observing ants. You can first have the child look at

Difficulty level: Low

From 3 years

Adult Supervision

some photos of ants at home, explain to them what they eat and how they live, so they can look for them with greater awareness. Once the child has found some ants, you can remind them to remain silent and watch them toil away. In the case of younger children, it's useful to explain to them what they are observing. You can then try placing a piece of bread near the ants and observe their reaction. Teach the child to respect these small and defenseless animals, not to hinder their work and to observe with curiosity how they can work in synergy.

Searching for a four-leafed clover

MATERIALS
A PAPER-MADE FOUR-LEAFED CLOVER,
A MAGNIFYING GLASS.

OBJECTIVES - Looking for a four-leafed clover is one of the best activities for practicing patience, perseverance and the child's ability to wait, as it requires asking them to look for a fairly rare object. In addition, it develops selective attention, stimulates observation and concentration, and exercises visual recognition.

HOW TO DO IT - First, get a photo of a four-leafed clover; print it and cut it out, so the child can get a good look at what a four-leaf clover looks like and how it's constructed; they can count the number of leaves, thus having the natural element they are looking for well impressed in their mind. Then take the child to a meadow, bringing along the paper four-leafed clover to find its duplicate amongst the many three-leafed clovers around. If you prefer, you can give the child a magnifying glass to give a greater emphasis to the research.

Immediately inform the child of the difficulty of finding a four-leafed clover and, therefore, how it requires a bit of luck. However, also tell them how important it is to look for difficult things, and how rewarding it can be to reach the results. In this case, the parent's role is to support the child, because they will soon grow tired of not finding it, will want to give up and conclude the activity quickly. Accept the fact that this can happen at any moment and on different occasions; the important thing is to encourage them not to give up, but rather to continue the search, hang in there, persevere and keep on looking even if the result is difficult to attain. This is an activity through which the child can come to emotionally understand the degree to which anticipation and patience are useful qualities in the attainment of objectives. And sooner or later the four-leafed clover will appear. Dry it and keep it in a frame as a tribute to this conquest.

Drawing from nature

Difficulty level: Low

From 2 years

Adult Supervision

OBJECTIVES - Drawing outside is very useful, mainly because it allows the child to experiment with the reality of what they reproduce rather than see it merely on a screen or printed on a page; they can actually touch the object, observe its details and understand its dimensions. It develops observation as well as focused and sustained attention, exercises drawing skills and perfects the knowledge of objects.

HOW TO DO IT - Choose a destination that is of interest to the child (a park, a garden, a road) and suggest that they pick out an attractive object and try to reproduce it on drawing paper. They can begin with a flower, for example, accurately observing its parts and appreciating the shades of their color and size. The child can choose to use the material with which they feel more comfortable: watercolors, pencils, felt-tip markers ... Give them as much time as they need; the precision and the perfection of the drawing do not matter. What does count is the child's ability to observe, detect details and have the patience to draw and redraw and reproduce one item at a time. With younger children, you can familiarize them with colors and nature, giving them a brush and making them paint with watercolors on stones or leaves, then using these as stamps on sheets of paper.

MATERIALS
A NOTEBOOK AND SHEETS OF DRAWING PAPER, PENCIL, ERASER, SHARPENER, COLORED PENCILS, FELT-TIP MARKERS, CHALK, TEMPERA PAINTS OR WATERCOLORS, 2 BRUSHES.

Outdoor gardening

Difficulty level: Low

From 2 years

Adult Supervision

MATERIALS

A PAIR OF GARDENING GLOVES, A RAKE, SOME SOIL, A POT, A WATERING CAN, A SHOVEL.

OBJECTIVES

Gardening enhances motor skills, precision, attention to movement and concentration and develops a sense of respect for the environment.

HOW TO DO IT

There are many outdoor gardening activities that children can perform. Such activities can be differentiated according to season. For example, in autumn, children can use a rake to collect leaves that have fallen from the trees. All you have to do is provide them with a rake and a bag for collecting leaves, teach them how to pick them from the ground, put them in a bag and discard the bag with the dry leaves. Other gardening activities may include repotting a plant, letting the child take the earth with their hands, sink their fingers into the soil, feel its moisture and feel how deep roots can be. Using rounded scissors, they can also snip dry leaves from a seedling.

Later on, you can give the child some soil, make them pour it into a flower pot and plant seeds to grow a plant.

Or you can give them a watering can and ask them to water the various plants, teaching them how to determine the amount of water, how to pour it, how to fill the watering can and how to empty it. You can also make them help you mow the grass, pick up the fresh-cut grass, gather it and throw it away. These activities can be conducted either in a private garden or in a public park.

Creating a "nature board"

MATERIALS
3 EGG CONTAINERS, VARIOUS NATURAL ELEMENTS, GLUE.

OBJECTIVES - Promote the child's curiosity and detailed observation; record information on the elements they find; stimulate vocabulary through the introduction of new and technical terms.

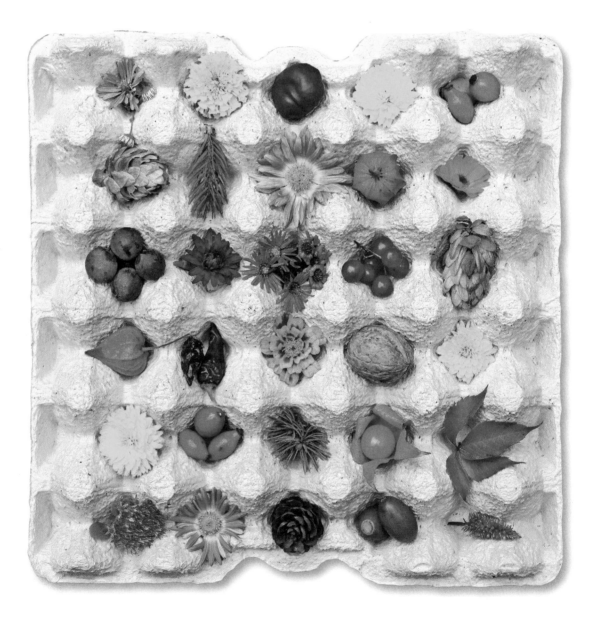

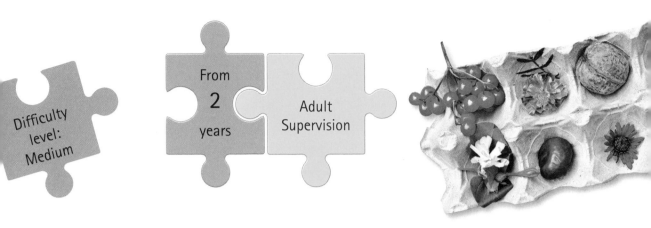

HOW TO DO IT - Take the egg containers and glue them on the long side to create a single board. You can choose whether to use their front or rear. You can build a variety of board types.

Figure out whether you'd prefer to devote your board to a specific theme (such as nature in a specific site or season, or elements of nature of an identical color, etc.) or whether you wish to place a variety of items in your board. Each time you go out, gather some items that you find interesting and place them in the egg containers. You can gather leaves, pine cones, pebbles, acorns, grasses, all kinds of flowers, berries, etc. ... For example, if you want to make a board about nature in autumn, you can collect dry leaves of various shape and color, chestnuts, meadow flowers, spice sprigs, fruit seeds. You can take items both from home and from outdoor locations. As you gradually add items, provide the child with information about what they are and what they are called, repeating their names several times. Make the child notice their colors, smells and texture. Once you have completed your board, ask the child to tell you what's on their nature board, making them repeat the names and information that you have passed on to them.

With younger children, you can simply get them to help you gather the elements and set them in the board while appreciating their sensory characteristics.

Building a bird house

MATERIALS

WOODEN BIRD HOUSE, OR 2 APPROXIMATELY 1.2" THICK WOODEN BOARDS FOR THE WALLS, WITH A RIGHT SIDE OF 8" AND A LEFT ONE (FOR THE SLOPING ROOF) MEASURING 10", AND A HEIGHT OF 6"; A 8" X 6" WOODEN BOARD FOR THE FRONT, WITH A HOLE MEASURING 1" IN DIAMETER; A 6" X 4" BOARD FOR THE BOTTOM, WITH 4 0.01"-WIDE HOLES; A 18" X 6" BOARD FOR THE REAR AND FINALLY, A PIECE OF WOOD MEASURING 9"X 6.7" FOR THE ROOF. WOODEN NAILS, HAMMER, BRUSH, PAINT.

OBJECTIVES - This is a complex activity that requires an adult's assistance, but is a great way to practice fine manual dexterity, designing, active planning and concentration.

From **3** years

Adult Supervision

Difficulty level: High

HOW TO DO IT - If you want to attract birds to your garden or terrace, building little houses for them is certainly a good way to invite them. Your child can get busy at keeping the house clean, refilling the water dish and ensuring that there's no shortage of seeds for the birds.

In order to figure out the size of your house, find out what birds live in your area. First choose the place where you will put it, as it must be in a position appropriate to the needs of the birds, which are delicate and suspicious animals. Therefore avoid places where the presence of man is constant, because this would chase them away. You can buy ready-made wooden houses and then have your child paint them. Alternatively, you can build it yourself by assembling wooden panels of suitable size for the birds you wish to host. Consider drilling an approximately 2" hole at the front for the birds to enter, and another 4 holes at its bottom to allow for

fluid drainage and the ventilation of the interior. You don't need to put any material inside the house, because the birds will provide all they need for their nest. To attract birds add a bowl of water to your garden, a feeder with seeds and wait. If you are patient, your birds will arrive!

Photographing and drawing clouds

MATERIALS
COLORED CRAYONS, PHOTO ALBUM WITH A4 PAGES,
ERASER, CAMERA.

OBJECTIVES - This activity deepens scientific knowledge, stimulates observation, develops concentration and exercises drawing skills.

HOW TO DO IT - Familiarizing your child with clouds means sensitizing them to their surrounding environment, making them understand the physical mechanisms through which clouds are created and stimulating their curiosity by capturing the clouds in a drawing or immortalizing them with a camera. First, dedicate some time at home to looking at clouds in illustrated or photography books, explaining to the child what they are made of and how it's possible for all of them to be different.

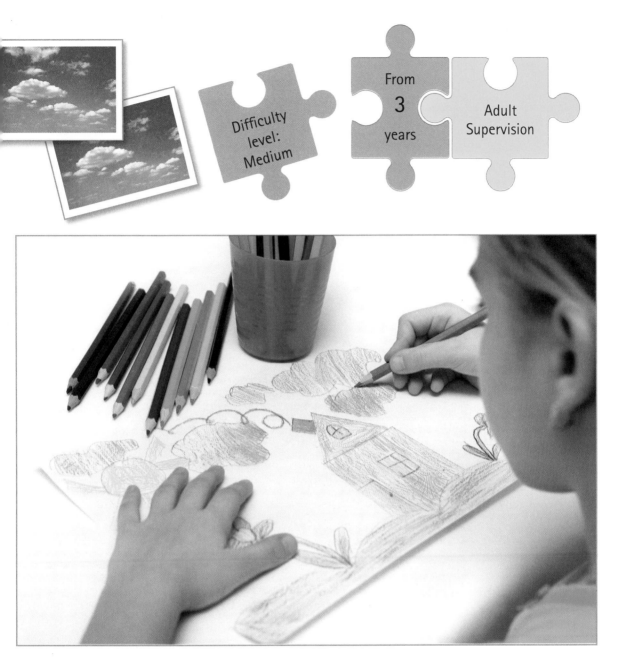

With older children, you can also go into detail by showing them categories of clouds, which the child will be able to recognize by observing them in real life.

Choose days when clouds are scattered and they have well-defined and recognizable shapes. Ask the child to look up at the sky and observe them. When they find one they like or that somehow catches their attention, prompt them to stop and draw it, copying it from reality. Alternatively, you can photograph it. Then put together an album with all the drawings or photos of clouds and browse through it together while trying to associate a form, a character and a general meaning to each cloud.

CHIARA PIRODDI - An Italian psychologist and expert in Neuropsychology specialized in Cognitive-Developmental Psychotherapy, Chiara Piroddi earned her degree in Psychology at the University of Pavia in 2007 and continued at the same institution as a Lecturer in Physiological Psychology and instructor in Practical Exercises in Neuropsychology. She did her training in the field at the Niguarda Ca' Granda hospital in Milan, where she has worked since 2008, gaining clinical experience with children of all ages with severe mental, psychological and learning disabilities. Ms Piroddi currently has a private practice as a psychotherapist for adults, parents and adolescents. She is the author and co-author of a number of scholarly publications in Neuropsychology and has written a series of books and boxes for White Star Kids entitled *Montessori, a World of Achievements*.

Graphic design
MARIA CUCCHI

PHOTO CREDITS